Holt Physics

SAT* Bellringer Workbook

Addresses Math and Verbal Skills

HOLT, RINEHART AND WINSTON

A Harcourt Education Company

Orlando • **Austin** • New York • San Diego • London

To the Teacher

Teachers in all disciplines are called upon to help prepare students for the SAT[*] reasoning test. As a science teacher, you are already targeting many of the same skills that your students will need in order to perform well on standardized tests. Using the SAT Bellringer Workbook, your students can assess their physics skills while preparing to take the SAT reasoning test.

The practice chapters in these transparencies are presented in a format similar to the SAT reasoning test. If your students are familiar with the test format, they may experience lower levels of anxiety and, therefore, perform better when faced with the actual test. Because the essays, reading selections, mathematical concepts, and science topics in this workbook mirror the physics content presented in the chapters of Holt Physics, students will remain focused on physics while preparing for tests in other disciplines.

Every item in each of the chapters is correlated to the National Science Education Standards for Science Content grades 9–12, and Unifying Concepts and Processes (UCP). In addition, items address math and verbal skills throughout the workbook. At the end of the workbook are answer sheets that can be used with each chapter. There is an answer key for each chapter, which includes correlations to all of the applicable National Science Education Standards for Science Content.

ISBN 13: 978-0-03-036852-3

IBSN 10: 0-03-036852-9

4 5 6 7 8 1431 15 14 13 12 11

4500291422

Table of Contents

Holt Physics: The Science of Physics
Essay

DIRECTIONS: The essay gives you an opportunity to show how effectively you can develop and express ideas. You should, therefore, take care to develop your ideas, present concepts logically and clearly, and use language precisely.

Your essay must be written on your own paper. You may use both sides of a single sheet of notebook paper. You will have enough space if you write on every line, avoid wide margins, and keep your handwriting to a reasonable size. Remember that people who are not familiar with your handwriting will read what you write. Try to write or print so that what you are writing is legible to those readers.

IMPORTANT REMINDERS:
- **A pencil is required for the essay.** An essay written in ink will receive a score of zero.
- **Do not write your essay in your test book.** You will receive credit only for what you write on a single sheet of notebook paper.
- **An off-topic essay will receive a score of zero.**

Think carefully about the concept presented in the following passage and the assignment below.

During a field experiment to determine the speed of a running rabbit, a scientist created the chart below, which shows distance and time measurements for the rabbit's motion along the straight section of a track.

Time (s)	Distance (m)
0.0	0.0
1.0	9.6
2.0	19.2
3.0	28.8
4.0	38.4

ASSIGNMENT: What is the rabbit's average speed along the section of track (expressed in units of kilometers per hour)? Is this speed constant or varying and how can you tell? How do significant figures play a role in the calculation for speed? How do unit conversions affect the number of significant figures in the answer? Plan and write a conclusion paragraph for a laboratory report in which you address these questions. Support your explanation with reasoning and examples taken from your reading, studies, experience, or observations.

Holt Physics: The Science of Physics
Mathematics

DIRECTIONS: In this section, solve each problem using any available space on the page for scratch work. Then decide which of the choices given is best and fill in the corresponding circle on the answer sheet.

NOTES:
1. The use of a calculator is permitted. All numbers used are real numbers.
2. Figures that accompany problems in this test are intended to provide information useful in solving the problems. They are drawn as accurately as possible EXCEPT when it is stated in a specific problem that the figure is not drawn to scale. All figures lie in a plane unless otherwise indicated.

Power	Metric Prefix	Abbreviation	Power	Metric Prefix	Abbreviation
10^{-18}	atto-	a	10^{-1}	deci-	d
10^{-15}	femto-	f	10^{1}	deka-	da
10^{-12}	pico-	p	10^{3}	kilo-	k
10^{-9}	nano-	n	10^{6}	mega-	M
10^{-6}	micro-	μ	10^{9}	giga-	G
10^{-3}	milli-	m	10^{12}	tera-	T
10^{-2}	centi-	c	10^{15}	peta-	P

Reference Information

1. A physicist filled a small hydraulic tube with 643 μL of fluid. How many liters is this?

   (A) 6.43×10^{-8} L

   (B) 6.43×10^{-6} L

   (C) 6.43×10^{-4} L

   (D) 6.43×10^{2} L

   (E) 6.43×10^{6} L

2. How many milligrams is 0.00997 kg of aluminum?

   (A) 9.97×10^{-9} mg

   (B) 9.97×10^{-2} mg

   (C) 9.97 mg

   (D) 9.97×10^{3} mg

   (E) 9.97×10^{6} mg

3. A molecular bond is 0.09584 nm in length. What is this length expressed in meters?

   (A) $9.584 \ 10^{-12}$ m

   (B) $9.584 \ 10^{-11}$ m

   (C) $9.584 \ 10^{-9}$ m

   (D) $9.584 \ 10^{-8}$ m

   (E) $9.584 \ 10^{-7}$ m

4. Memory storage in a laboratory computer is measured in bytes (B). How many 17 kB files will fit on a 51 GB hard drive?

   (A) 3.0×10^{3}

   (B) 3.0×10^{6}

   (C) 3.0×10^{9}

   (D) 3.0×10^{12}

   (E) 3.0×10^{27}

GO ON TO THE NEXT PAGE

| Mathematics *continued*

5. How many 4.3-nm wires can fit side-by-side across a distance of 12.47 cm?

   (A) 2.9×10^7

   (B) 2.9×10^8

   (C) 2.9×10^9

   (D) 2.9×10^{11}

   (E) 2.9×10^{18}

6. Which answer follows the correct rules for significant figures on the following operation?
   126.05 cm + 3.367 cm = ?

   (A) 129 cm

   (B) 129.4 cm

   (C) 129.42 cm

   (D) 129.417 cm

   (E) 129.4170 cm

7. Which answer follows the correct rules for significant figures on the following operation?
   42.4 mL × 1.5 = ?

   (A) 60 mL

   (B) 64 mL

   (C) 63.6 mL

   (D) 63.60 mL

   (E) 63.600 mL

8. Which answer follows the correct rules for significant figures on the following operation?
   4200.5 kg ÷ 32.5 kg = ?

   (A) 130

   (B) 129

   (C) 129.2

   (D) 129.25

   (E) 129.246

GO ON TO THE NEXT PAGE

Questions 9 and 10 are based on the following graph of laboratory data.

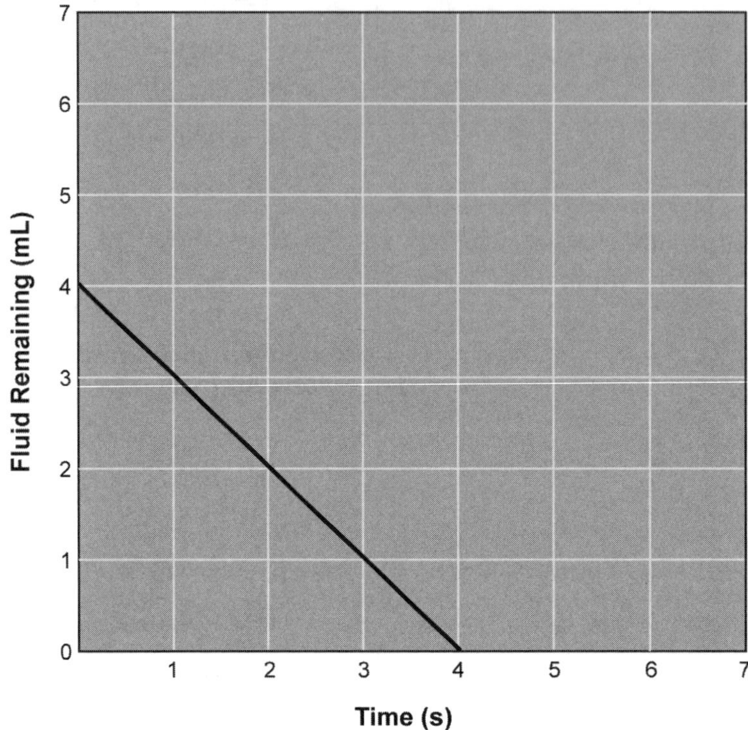

9. Which set of data points below best matches the graph above?

   (A) 0 s, 0 mL; 1 s, 0 mL; 2 s, 0 mL; 3 s, 0 mL; 4 s, 0 mL

   (B) 0 s, 1 mL; 1 s, 2 mL; 2 s, 3 mL; 3 s, 4 mL; 4 s, 5 mL

   (C) 0 s, 3 mL; 1 s, 2 mL; 2 s, 1 mL; 3 s, 0 mL; 4 s, 4 mL

   (D) 0 s, 4 mL; 1 s, 3 mL; 2 s, 2 mL; 3 s, 1 mL; 4 s, 0 mL

   (E) 0 s, 4 mL; 1 s, 4 mL; 2 s, 4 mL; 3 s, 4 mL; 4 s, 4 mL

10. If F represents the fluid remaining in milliliters and t represents the time in seconds, which equation below best matches the data in the graph above?

   (A) $F = 4 - t$

   (B) $F = 4 + t$

   (C) $t = 4 + F$

   (D) $t = 4F$

   (E) $F = 4t$

GO ON TO THE NEXT PAGE

Holt Physics: The Science of Physics
Sentence Completion

DIRECTIONS: For each question in this section, select the best answer from among the choices given and fill in the corresponding circle on the answer sheet.

11. Mechanics is the study of motion and its causes and interactions between ______.

    (A) waves

    (B) objects

    (C) light and energy

    (D) electricity and light

    (E) heat and temperature

12. ______ is the study of the behavior of submicroscopic particles, such as protons and electrons.

    (A) electromagnetism

    (B) optics

    (C) relativity

    (D) thermodynamics

    (E) quantum mechanics

13. A ______ is a set of particles or interacting components considered to be a distinct physical entity for the purpose of study.

    (A) controlled experiment

    (B) hypothesis

    (C) model

    (D) system

    (E) variable

14. A scientist increased the ______ of her measurements by using a micrometer instead of a meterstick.

    (A) accuracy

    (B) errors

    (C) precision

    (D) significant figures

    (E) uncertainty

15. A measurement that reflects poor ______ involves errors that can often be corrected, while one that has low ______ cannot be made more exact.

    (A) precision . . values

    (B) technique . . values

    (C) precision . . accuracy

    (D) accuracy . . precision

    (E) technique . . accuracy

Holt Physics: The Science of Physics
Reading Passage

The passage below is followed by questions based on its content. Answer the questions on the basis of what is <u>stated</u> or <u>implied</u> in the passage. For each question in this section, select the best answer from among the choices given and fill in the corresponding circle on the answer sheet.

Questions 16–20 are based on the following passage.

    When performing calculations that involve several unit conversions, dimensional analysis can help you keep track of units. Dimensional analysis is a

5   method of mathematical notation that shows how the dimensions, or units, of different quantities are multiplied together in a calculation so that matching units cancel out to reveal the correct units of

10   the answer. You can use dimensional analysis to keep track of units in physics equations, even when no unit conversions are needed. It can also help you carry out complicated unit conversions that involve

15   several steps.

    To perform a unit conversion, you must find the proper conversion factor. A conversion factor is a ratio that shows how two units are related. For example,

20   there are 100 cm in a meter. This relationship provides two conversion factors: 100 cm/1 m and 1 m/100 cm.

    When converting from centimeters to meters, you multiply the quantity

25   expressed in centimeters by the second conversion factor (1 m/100 cm) so that the centimeter units cancel out, as shown in the following example:

$$(55 \text{ cm})\left(\frac{1 \text{ m}}{100 \text{ cm}}\right) = 0.55 \text{ m}$$

30   When converting from meters to centimeters, you multiply the quantity expressed in meters by the first

conversion factor (100 cm/1 m) so that the meter units cancel out, as shown in

35   the following example:

$$(2.1 \text{ m})(\frac{100 \text{ cm}}{1 \text{ m}}) = 210 \text{ cm}$$

    When performing a conversion that involves several steps, or when using a formula and simultaneously performing a

40   unit conversion, you might cancel out more than one type of unit. For example, if you are given a distance expressed in kilometers and a time expressed in minutes, you can use a single equation to

45   determine the speed expressed in units of meters per second. The following example involves a calculation of speed and a unit conversion within the same dimensional analysis setup:

50   Given distance: 0.92 km
Given time: 8.93 min
Desired units for answer: m/s

$$\left(\frac{0.92 \text{ km}}{8.93 \text{ min}}\right)\left(\frac{1000 \text{ m}}{1 \text{ km}}\right)\left(\frac{1 \text{ min}}{60 \text{ s}}\right) = 1.7 \text{ m/s}$$

    Notice that you still must follow the

55   rules of significant figures when performing your calculations. The answer above reflects the number of significant figures in the least precise quantity. Conversion factor units are often not

60   counted in significant figure calculations, because they represent exact relationships that have an infinite number of significant figures.

GO ON TO THE NEXT PAGE

Reading Passage *continued*

16. The word "dimensional" mentioned in line 4 refers to

    (A) physics

    (B) ratios

    (C) shapes

    (D) space

    (E) units

17. According to lines 16–19, what type of mathematical expression is a conversion factor?

    (A) equation

    (B) exponent

    (C) quantity

    (D) ratio

    (E) unit

18. The sample calculations in lines 29 and 36 differ in

    (A) the SI base-unit used

    (B) the conversion factor used

    (C) whether dimensional analysis is used

    (D) the type of quantity that is expressed (e.g. length or volume)

    (E) number of significant figures that appear in the answer

19. The author's use of text that is struck out in lines 29, 36, and 53 serves primarily to

    (A) emphasize important data

    (B) show the canceling of units

    (C) demarcate units that are not SI

    (D) illustrate an incorrect calculation

    (E) demonstrate how mistakes and their corrections should be recorded

20. What is the main idea of the final paragraph in the passage?

    (A) Follow the rules for significant figures even with calculations involving conversion factors.

    (B) Significant figures are not usually counted in dimensional analysis calculations.

    (C) Answers always reflect the number of significant figures in the least precise quantity used in a calculation.

    (D) Dimensional analysis shows how the units of different quantities are multiplied together in a calculation.

    (E) Significant figures are the digits in a measurement that are known with certainty plus the first uncertain digit.

GO ON TO THE NEXT PAGE

Holt Physics: The Science of Physics
Improving Sentences

DIRECTIONS: For each question in this section, select the best answer from among the choices given and fill in the corresponding circle on the answer sheet.

Part of each sentence in items 21 and 22 is underlined. Below each sentence are five ways of phrasing the underlined material. Choice A repeats the original phrasing; the other four choices are different. Choose the answer you think produces the most accurate sentence.

21. A controlled experiment tests <u>as many factors as possible</u> by comparing a control group and an experimental group.

   (A) as many factors as possible

   (B) only one factor at a time

   (C) only factors that are identical

   (D) two or more factors at a time

   (E) only factors that involve measurements

22. When adding two quantities with different numbers of significant figures, the result must have the same number of significant figures as <u>the least precise of the two quantities</u>.

   (A) the least precise of the two quantities

   (B) the most precise of the two quantities

   (C) the quantity with the smallest number of digits to the left of the decimal point

   (D) the quantity with the smallest number of digits to the right of the decimal point

   (E) the sum of the significant figures of the two quantities

Each sentence in items 23 and 24 contains either a single error or no error at all. If the sentence contains an error, choose the one underlined part that must be changed to make the sentence correct. If the sentence is correct, select choice E.

23. In a procedure that has a(n) <u>method</u>
                          A

   error, some measurements are taken using

   one <u>method</u>, while other measurements
       B

   are taken using another, whereas a

   procedure that has a(n) <u>instrumental</u>
                         C

   error simply includes faulty <u>equipment</u>.
                            D

   <u>No error</u>
    E

24. A(n) <u>order-of-magnitude</u> calculation
              A
   involves determining the power of <u>ten</u>
                          B

   that is closest to the <u>hypothesized</u>
                      C

   numerical value of the <u>quantity</u>.
                   D

   <u>No error</u>
    E

Holt Physics: Motion in One Dimension
Essay

DIRECTIONS: The essay gives you an opportunity to show how effectively you can develop and express ideas. You should, therefore, take care to develop your ideas, present concepts logically and clearly, and use language precisely.

Your essay must be written on your own paper. You may use both sides of a single sheet of notebook paper. You will have enough space if you write on every line, avoid wide margins, and keep your handwriting to a reasonable size. Remember that people who are not familiar with your handwriting will read what you write. Try to write or print so that what you are writing is legible to those readers.

IMPORTANT REMINDERS:
- **A pencil is required for the essay.** An essay written in ink will receive a score of zero.
- **Do not write your essay in your test book.** You will receive credit only for what you write on a single sheet of notebook paper.
- **An off-topic essay will receive a score of zero.**

Think carefully about the concept presented in the following passage and the assignment below.

A scientist measured the distance an object traveled along a straight path as a function of time. The graph below shows her data.

Distance Versus Time

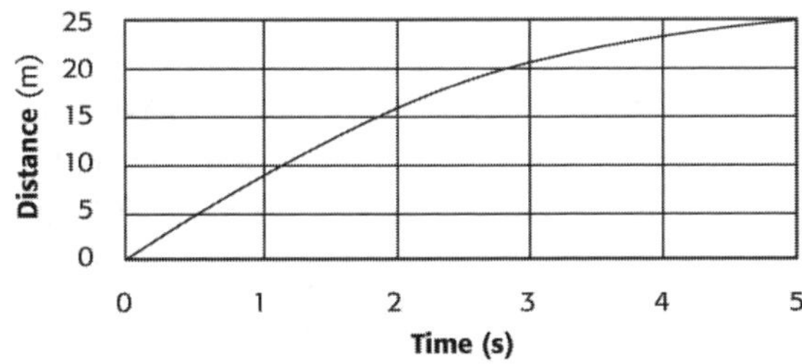

ASSIGNMENT: What does the slope of the line tell you at each point in the graph? Describe the motion of the object in terms of its velocity and acceleration? Plan and write an essay in which you address these questions. Support your explanation with reasoning and examples taken from your reading, studies, experience, or observations.

Holt Physics: Motion in One Dimension
Mathematics

DIRECTIONS: In this section, solve each problem using any available space on the page for scratch work. Then decide which of the choices given is best and fill in the corresponding circle on the answer sheet.

NOTES:
1. The use of a calculator is permitted. All numbers used are real numbers.
2. Figures that accompany problems in this test are intended to provide information useful in solving the problems. They are drawn as accurately as possible EXCEPT when it is stated in a specific problem that the figure is not drawn to scale. All figures lie in a plane unless otherwise indicated.

Reference Information

Displacement

$$\Delta x = x_f - x_i$$

Average Velocity

$$v_{avg} = \frac{\Delta x}{\Delta t} = \frac{x_f - x_i}{t_f - t_i}$$

Average Acceleration

$$a_{avg} = \frac{\Delta v}{\Delta t} = \frac{v_f - v_i}{t_f - t_i}$$

Displacement with Constant Acceleration

$$\Delta x = \frac{1}{2}\left(v_i + v_f\right)\Delta t$$

Velocity with Constant Acceleration

$$v_f = v_i + a\Delta t$$

Displacement with Constant Acceleration

$$\Delta x = v_i\Delta t + \frac{1}{2}a\left(\Delta t\right)^2$$

Final Velocity after Any Displacement

$$v_f^{\,2} = v_i^{\,2} + 2a\Delta x$$

1. A girl rides her bike with an average velocity of 15.2 km/h northward. If it takes her 25 min to ride to her friend's house, what is her displacement?

   (A) 1.6 km

   (B) 3.8 km

   (C) 6.3 km

   (D) 7.6 km

   (E) 380 km

2. A man hikes 6.6 km north along a straight path with an average velocity of 4.2 km/h to the north. He rests at a bench for 15 min. Then, he hikes 3.8 km north with an average velocity of 5.1 km/h to the north. How long does the total hike last?

   (A) 1.1 h

   (B) 2.0 h

   (C) 2.2 h

   (D) 2.3 h

   (E) 2.6 h

GO ON TO THE NEXT PAGE

| Mathematics *continued*

Questions 3 and 4 are based on the following graph that shows the distance an object traveled along a straight path as a function of time.

Distance Versus Time

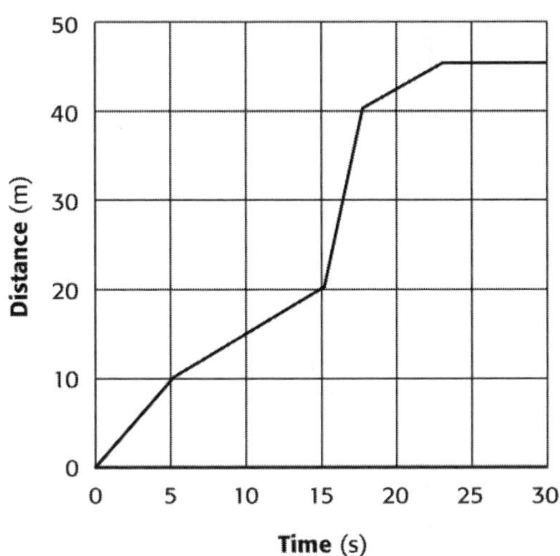

3. During which of the following time periods did the object travel at a constant velocity?

   (A) 0–5 s

   (B) 0–15 s

   (C) 15–20 s

   (D) 20–25 s

   (E) 20–30 s

4. At which time did the object experience a positive acceleration?

   (A) 5 s

   (B) 15 s

   (C) 15.5 s

   (D) 22.5 s

   (E) 25 s

5. With an average acceleration of 1.5 m/s^2, how long will it take a driver to accelerate from a complete stop to 25 km/h?

   (A) 3.6 s

   (B) 4.6 s

   (C) 17 s

   (D) 60 s

   (E) 280 s

6. A cheetah runs at a steady velocity of 60 km/h (16.7 m/s). Over a period of 5.0 s, the cheetah increases its pace to 95 km/h (26.4 m/s). What is the average acceleration of the cheetah over this period?

   (A) 1.9 m/s^2

   (B) 3.5 m/s^2

   (C) 7.0 m/s^2

   (D) 9.7 m/s^2

   (E) 48 m/s^2

7. An elevator accelerates uniformly from rest to a speed of 2.5 m/s in 12 s. What is the distance the elevator travels during this time?

   (A) 1.3 m

   (B) 4.8 m

   (C) 14 m

   (D) 15 m

   (E) 30 m

GO ON TO THE NEXT PAGE

| Mathematics *continued*

Questions 8 and 9 are based on the following illustration, which shows the positions of a feather and a rock over time as they fall in a vacuum. NOTE: Figure is not to scale.

VELOCITIES OF FALLING OBJECTS

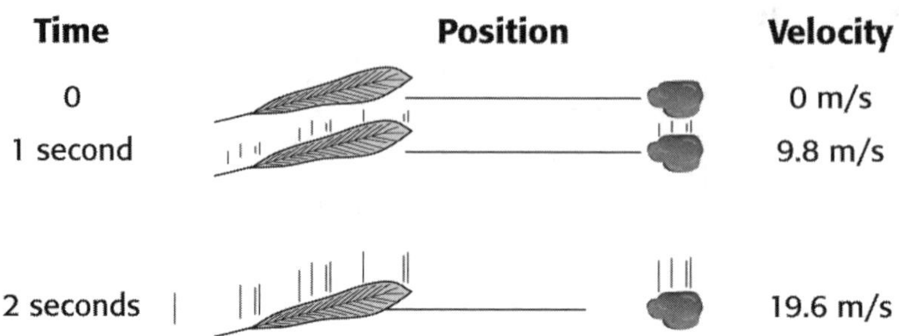

8. What is the feather's average acceleration during the first 2 s?

   (A) 4.9 m/s^2

   (B) 9.8 m/s^2

   (C) 14.7 m/s^2

   (D) 19.6 m/s^2

   (E) 39.2 m/s^2

9. If the feather continued to fall at this same acceleration, what would its velocity be after 20 s?

   (A) 2 m/s

   (B) 20 m/s

   (C) 200 m/s

   (D) 2,000 m/s

   (E) 20,000 m/s

10. A boat with an initial speed of 5.0 m/s accelerates at a uniform rate of 1.2 m/s^2 for 5.0 s. What is the final speed of the boat during this time?

    (A) 6.0 m/s   (D) 26 m/s

    (B) 6.2 m/s   (E) 31 m/s

    (C) 11 m/s

11. A child on a tricycle starts from rest, uniformly accelerating at a rate of 0.35 m/s^2. What is the velocity of the tricycle after it has traveled 750 cm?

    (A) 0.72 m/s

    (B) 2.3 m/s

    (C) 2.6 m/s

    (D) 5.2 m/s

    (E) 23 m/s

12. A clown throws a juggling pin upward with an initial velocity of 10.5 m/s. How long will the pin take to return to its starting point?

    (A) 0.934 s

    (B) 1.07 s

    (C) 1.87 s

    (D) 2.14 s

    (E) 19.6 s

Holt Physics: Motion in One Dimension
Sentence Completion

DIRECTIONS: For each question in this section, select the best answer from among the choices given and fill in the corresponding circle on the answer sheet.

13. In describing the motion of an object it is often helpful to identify a ______, which allows you to describe its motion relative to that of another object.

    (A) acceleration

    (B) average velocity

    (C) frame of reference

    (D) instantaneous velocity

    (E) speed

14. Average acceleration can by found by determining the ______ of the straight line connecting the initial and final points on a graph of an object's velocity versus time.

    (A) endpoint

    (B) midpoint

    (C) slope

    (D) starting point

    (E) thickness

15. The constant acceleration directed toward the center of Earth exerted on all objects on Earth's surface is called ______.

    (A) relative motion

    (B) free-fall velocity

    (C) instantaneous velocity

    (D) instantaneous acceleration

    (E) acceleration due to gravity

16. An object in free fall experiences a constant ______.

    (A) acceleration

    (B) displacement

    (C) position

    (D) speed

    (E) velocity

Holt Physics: Motion in One Dimension
Reading Passage

The passage and figures below are followed by questions based on their content. Answer the questions on the basis of what is <u>stated</u> or <u>implied</u> in the passage. For each question in this section, select the best answer from the choices given and fill in the corresponding circle on the answer sheet.

Figure 1

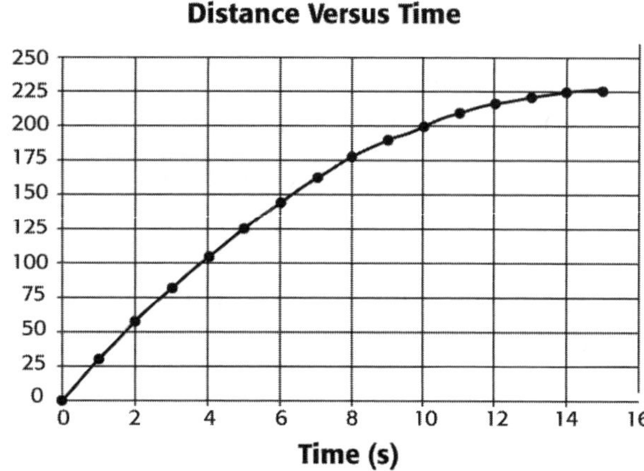

Figure 2

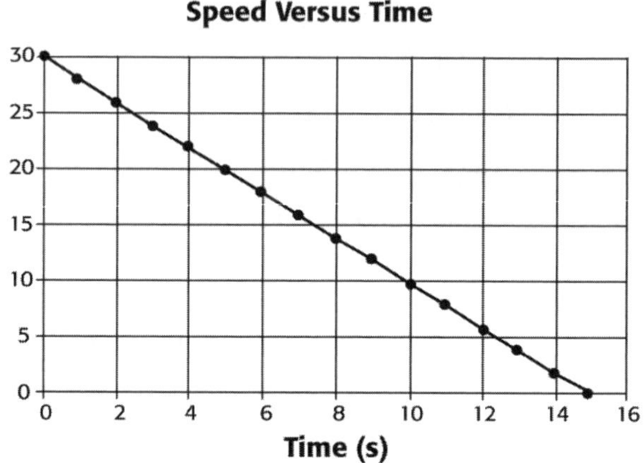

Questions 17–20 are based on the following passage.

Jin and Beth were doing an experiment in science class using a toy car. They attached a strip of paper tape to the car and allowed the paper tape to pass *Line* through a recording timer. As the car 5 moved, it pulled the paper tape through the timer. The recording timer made dots on the paper tape at regular time intervals. Jin and Beth then collected data about 10 the speed of the car by measuring the distance between dots on the paper tape. During one trial of the experiment, Jin pushed the car along the floor for 225 cm.

Line The car pulled the tape through the 15 recording timer as it moved.

Beth and Jin analyzed the dots on the tape and made the graph shown in Figure 1 from their data. Then, Beth was able to use the data in Figure 1 to create Figure 2.

17. Lines 12–13 suggest that the *y*-axis of Figure 1 should be labeled

(A) Acceleration (m/s^2)

(B) Distance (cm)

(C) Distance (m)

(D) Speed (cm/s)

(E) Speed (m/s)

GO ON TO THE NEXT PAGE

Reading Passage *continued*

18. According to lines 4–11, where did the data points on the graph come from?

   (A) measurements Beth made by looking at a stopwatch

   (B) data collected by a light-sensitive computer probe

   (C) times estimated by Jin as the toy car passed strips of paper tape

   (D) dots made by a recording timer on the paper tape at regular intervals

   (E) ink traces the car made with its wheels as it traveled along the paper tape

19. According to lines 16–19, how are Figure 1 and Figure 2 related?

   (A) They show data from two different trials of the same toy car.

   (B) They show data from similar trials using two different toy cars.

   (C) They show data from two different teams of students in the science class.

   (D) The information in Figure 1 was used to calculate the data shown in Figure 2.

   (E) The information in Figure 2 was used to calculate the data shown in Figure 1.

20. How do the slopes of the lines in each figure relate to the motion of the toy car?

   (A) The slopes of the lines in both figures show velocity.

   (B) The slopes of the lines in both figures show displacement.

   (C) The slopes of the lines in both figures show acceleration.

   (D) The slope of the line in Figure 1 shows acceleration, while the slope of the line in Figure 2 shows velocity.

   (E) The slope of the line in Figure 1 shows velocity, while the slope of the line in Figure 2 shows acceleration.

Holt Physics: Motion in One Dimension
Improving Sentences

DIRECTIONS: For each question in this section, select the best answer from among the choices given and fill in the corresponding circle on the answer sheet.

Part of each sentence in items 21 and 22 is underlined. Below each sentence are five ways of phrasing the underlined material. Choice A repeats the original phrasing; the other four choices are different. Choose the answer you think produces the most accurate sentence.

21. For a ball thrown into the air, its acceleration is 9.81 m/s^2 downward, <u>except at the peak</u> where the velocity is zero.

    (A) except at the peak

    (B) even at the peak

    (C) only at the peak

    (D) unless it comes to a peak

    (E) unless it falls back to its starting point

22. For all objects on Earth's surface, free-fall acceleration is <u>dependent on mass</u>.

    (A) dependent on mass

    (B) dependent on volume

    (C) the same, regardless of mass

    (D) dependent on frame of reference

    (E) dependent on distance of travel

Each sentence in items 23 and 24 contains either a single error or no error at all. If the sentence contains an error, choose the one underlined part that must be changed to make the sentence correct. If the sentence is correct, select choice E.

23. On a graph of speed versus time, a <u>positive</u> slope indicates <u>an increase</u> in velocity, while a <u>negative</u> slope indicates <u>a decrease</u> in velocity. <u>No error</u>

    A   B   C   D   E

24. The <u>slope</u> of a straight line drawn from an object's <u>initial position</u> to its <u>final position</u> is called the object's <u>displacement</u>. <u>No error</u>

    A   B   C   D   E

Holt Physics: Two-Dimensional Motion and Vectors
Essay

DIRECTIONS: The essay gives you an opportunity to show how effectively you can develop and express ideas. You should, therefore, take care to develop your ideas, present concepts logically and clearly, and use language precisely.

Your essay must be written on your own paper. You may use both sides of a single sheet of notebook paper. You will have enough space if you write on every line, avoid wide margins, and keep your handwriting to a reasonable size. Remember that people who are not familiar with your handwriting will read what you write. Try to write or print so that z you are writing is legible to those readers.

IMPORTANT REMINDERS:

- **A pencil is required for the essay.** An essay written in ink will receive a score of zero.
- **Do not write your essay in your test book.** You will receive credit only for what you write on a single sheet of notebook paper.
- **An off-topic essay will receive a score of zero.**

Think carefully about the concept presented in the following passage and the assignment below.

At the county fair, Javier walked 300 m north along the aisles of booths. He then walked about 150 m east, where he ran into a friend. In all, he had walked 450 m. His final position was situated approximately 335 m north by northeast from his starting position.

ASSIGNMENT: How would you describe Javier's walk in terms of scalars, vectors, and resultants? Plan and write an essay in which you address this question, defining the appropriate vocabulary words. Support your explanation with reasoning and examples taken from your reading, studies, experience, or observations.

Holt Physics: Two-Dimensional Motion and Vectors
Mathematics

DIRECTIONS: In this section, solve each problem using any available space on the page for scratch work. Then decide which of the choices given is best and fill in the corresponding circle on the answer sheet.

NOTES:

1. The use of a calculator is permitted. All numbers used are real numbers.
2. Figures that accompany problems in this test are intended to provide information useful in solving the problems. They are drawn as accurately as possible EXCEPT when it is stated in a specific problem that the figure is not drawn to scale. All figures lie in a plane unless otherwise indicated.

Reference Information

Pythagorean Theorem

$$c^2 = a^2 + b^2$$

Tangent Function for Right Triangles

$$\tan \theta = \frac{\text{opp}}{\text{adj}}$$

Sine Function for Right Triangles

$$\sin \theta = \frac{\text{opp}}{\text{hyp}}$$

Cosine Function for Right Triangles

$$\cos \theta = \frac{\text{adj}}{\text{hyp}}$$

Horizontal Motion of a Projectile

$$v_x = v_{x,i} = \text{constant}$$
$$\Delta x = v_x \Delta t$$

Horizontal Motion of a Projectile that Falls from Rest

$$v_{y,f} = a_y \Delta t$$
$$v_{y,f}^2 = 2a_y \Delta y$$
$$\Delta y = \frac{1}{2} a_y (\Delta t)^2$$

Projectiles Launched at an Angle

$$v_x = v_{x,i} = v_i \cos \theta = \text{constant}$$
$$\Delta x = (v_i \cos \theta)\Delta t$$
$$v_{y,f} = v_i \sin \theta + a_y \Delta t$$
$$v_{y,f}^2 = v_i^2 (\sin \theta)^2 + 2a_y \Delta y$$
$$\Delta y = (v_i \sin \theta)\Delta t + \frac{1}{2} a_y (\Delta t)^2$$

1. A train engineer drives a train 235 km north along a straight track. Then he drives the train back south 126 km. Finally, he drives north again 45.0 km to his final destination. What is the engineer's total displacement?

   (A) 64.0 km to the north

   (B) 109 km to the south

   (C) 154 km to the north

   (D) 190 km to the south

   (E) 406 km to the north

2. A scout hikes 2.35 km east of a campsite. He takes a break for lunch and then hikes another 1.25 km north of the location where he ate lunch. What distance is the scout from the campsite?

   (A) 1.10 km

   (B) 2.66 km

   (C) 3.60 km

   (D) 7.08 km

   (E) 13.0 km

GO ON TO THE NEXT PAGE

Questions 3–4 are based on the following illustration of displacement vectors A and B, which each have a magnitude of 8.00 cm.

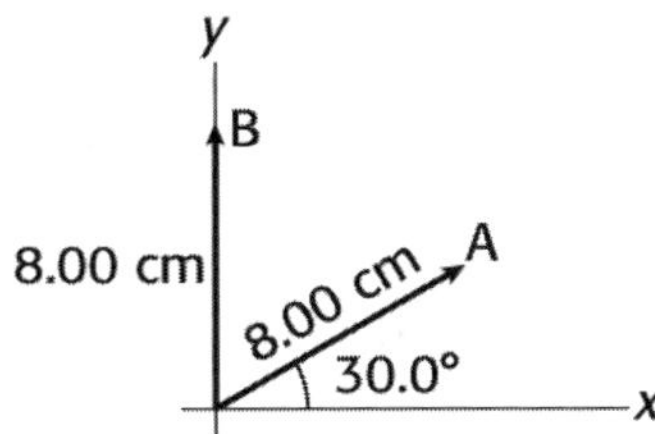

3. What is **A** + **B**?

   (A) 4.00 cm at 30.0° above the *x*- axis

   (B) 6.93 cm at 30.0° above the *x*- axis

   (C) 8.00 cm at 30.0° above the *x*- axis

   (D) 12.0 cm at 60.0° above the *x*- axis

   (E) 13.9 cm at 60.0° above the *x*- axis

4. What is **A** − **B**?

   (E) 13.9 cm at 60.0° below the *x*- axis

   (A) 1.07 cm at 30.0° below the *x*- axis

   (B) 4.00 cm at 30.0° below the *x*- axis

   (C) 8.00 cm at 30.0° below the *x*- axis

   (D) 12.0 cm at 60.0° below the *x*- axis

5. A squirrel climbs up to the top of a 6.2 m post. Then he crawls back to the ground via a rope that extends from the top of the post to the ground at an angle 35.0° from the post. At the end of its journey, how far is the squirrel from the base of the post?

   (A) 3.8 m

   (B) 4.3 m

   (C) 10 m

   (D) 41 m

   (E) 80 m

6. A woman pushes a cart up a ramp with a 20.0° incline. If the cart has a constant speed of 0.54 m/s, what are the horizontal and vertical components of the cart's velocity?

   (A) 0.20 m/s and 0.18 m/s

   (B) 0.51 m/s and 0.18 m/s

   (C) 0.51 m/s and 0.20 m/s

   (D) 1.48 m/s and 0.57 m/s

   (E) 1.58 m/s and 0.57 m/s

7. A roller skate rolls off a 2.50 m high ledge and lands on the ground 1.25 m away from the base of the ledge. How fast was the roller skate rolling?

   (A) 1.75 m/s

   (B) 3.92 m/s

   (C) 4.90 m/s

   (D) 7.82 m/s

   (E) 19.6 m/s

8. A soccer ball is kicked off a bridge with a height of 36 m. The ball travels 25 m horizontally before it hits the pavement below. What was the soccer ball's speed when it was first kicked?

   (A) 2.5 m/s

   (B) 3.7 m/s

   (C) 6.8 m/s

   (D) 9.2 m/s

   (E) 16 m/s

GO ON TO THE NEXT PAGE

Mathematics *continued*

9. A woman throws the weighted end of a rope across a river to a friend located on the opposite bank. She throws it with a velocity of 9.5 m/s at an angle of 30° relative to the ground. Her friend catches it at the same height it was thrown. How long was the rope end in the air before her friend caught it?

   (A) 0.48 s

   (B) 0.97 s

   (C) 5.06 s

   (D) 8.22 s

   (E) 16.45 s

10. A marble at the front of a truck bed traveling at 21 m/s relative to the highway rolls toward the back of the truck bed with a speed of 7 m/s relative to the truck bed. What is the velocity of the marble relative to the highway?

   (A) 3 m/s opposite the direction of the truck

   (B) 14 m/s in the direction of the truck

   (C) 18 m/s opposite the direction of the truck

   (D) 28 m/s in the direction of the truck

   (E) 147 m/s opposite the direction of the truck

11. A boy in a canoe paddles upriver at a speed of 1.4 m/s relative to the water. The water flows downriver at a speed of 1.4 m/s relative to the riverbed. How fast does the boy's canoe appear to move when viewed by an observer standing on the riverbank?

   (A) 0 m/s

   (B) 1.4 m/s up the river

   (C) 1.4 m/s down the river

   (D) 2.8 m/s up the river

   (E) 2.8 m/s down the river

12. A grocer rolls a can across a moving conveyor belt on a counter. If the can is rolled due south with a speed of 0.25 m/s relative to the counter and the conveyor belt's velocity is 0.55 m/s to the east, what will the can's velocity relative to the counter be?

   (A) 0.40 at 63° south of east

   (B) 0.60 at 24° south of east

   (C) 0.60 at 27° south of east

   (D) 0.80 at 30° south of east

   (E) 0.80 at 45° south of east

Holt Physics: Two-Dimensional Motion and Vectors
Sentence Completion

DIRECTIONS: For each question in this section, select the best answer from among the choices given and fill in the corresponding circle on the answer sheet.

13. A scalar has ______, while a vector has both magnitude and ______.
    (A) quantity . . units
    (B) scale . . quantity
    (C) direction . . units
    (D) magnitude . . direction
    (E) direction . . quantity

14. A vector that represents the sum of two or more vectors is a ______.
    (A) scalar
    (B) projectile
    (C) resultant
    (D) vertical component
    (E) horizontal component

15. The Pythagorean theorem states that for any right triangle, the square of the ______ equals the sum of the squares of the other two sides of the triangle.
    (A) adjacent side
    (B) cosine angle
    (C) hypotenuse
    (D) opposite side
    (E) tangent angle

16. Velocity measurements depend on the ______ the observer.
    (A) mass of
    (B) origin of
    (C) frame of reference of
    (D) time of day detected by
    (E) force of gravity acting on

The passages below are followed by questions based on their content; questions following a pair of related passages may also be based on the relationship between the paired passages. Answer the questions on the basis of what is <u>stated</u> or <u>implied</u> in the passages. For each question in this section, select the best answer from the choices given and fill in the corresponding circle on the answer sheet.

Questions 17–18 are based on the following passage.

When an archer uses a bow to shoot an arrow at a target that is far away, he or she will direct the arrow slightly higher than the target's height. In this way, the
Line archer can account for the vertical
5 displacement of the arrow due to the force of gravity. Experienced archers can estimate the amount of vertical displacement they must account for
10 when aiming for a target located at a given distance and shooting an arrow at a given velocity.

Archers must consider more than just the projectile motion of the arrow. They
15 must also take into account any horizontal displacement due to wind. If an archer detects a strong wind coming from one direction, he or she must aim to the side of the target (toward the wind) to
20 compensate for its force on the arrow.

17. According to the passage, what two kinds of displacement must an archer consider?
   (A) vertical displacement of the wind and horizontal displacement of gravity
   (B) vertical displacement of gravity and horizontal displacement of the wind
   (C) vertical and horizontal displacement of the arrow
   (D) vertical and horizontal displacement of the target
   (E) vertical displacement of the arrow and horizontal displacement of the target

18. Lines 14–16 suggest that the word "projectile motion" includes
   (A) a vertical component due to gravity
   (B) a horizontal component due to gravity
   (C) a vertical component due to launch velocity
   (D) a horizontal component due to wind velocity
   (E) a vertical component due to wind velocity

GO ON TO THE NEXT PAGE

Reading Passages *continued*

Questions 19–20 are based on the following passage.

Early that morning, Jonah met Janet at her house for their weekly walk. It was a beautiful day. The sky was gray, but
Line brightly illuminated, generating a gentle
5 glow that brought out a new vibrancy in the spring blooms.

"Let's take a new route," said Janet. "I want to see how Mrs. Garcia's rose garden looks now that it is May."
10 "That's a great idea," said Jonah. And, as he swung open the front gate, he startled a giant crow that had been perched on a nearby post. The two friends stepped back in surprise. As the great bird
15 took off in flight, Janet commented on a strange glint in its beak.

"I think it had something metal in its mouth!" she cried. "I wonder what it was, and I wonder if he stole it!"
20 They walked 8 blocks north and then 6 blocks east, where they paused for a brief rest on a small bench near a pond. Then they continued their walk, going 2 blocks south and 9 blocks east, arriving at
25 their anticipated destination.

The rose garden was dancing with color. Each row of bushes glowed with petals of a different shade. Some were solid pinks, whites, yellows, and reds,
30 while others had pale bases that blushed into rosy tips. All of them emitted an intoxicating fragrance.

As they headed away from the rose garden, Janet spotted the large crow again, this time alit a small stone statue.
35 "It looks like our friend beat us here," she said.

"I think it is likely he took a very different route," said Jonah. "In fact, I'd say he traveled here 'as the crow flies'

40 —that is, taking a direct route." Janet giggled at this silly remark.

Both friends observed the funny creature with quiet interest. The crow peered back at them cautiously. Then, he
45 picked up the very same metal object he had before and flew away to a safer roost.

19. According to the description in lines 20–25, if each block is exactly the same length, what is the approximate magnitude of the resultant displacement of their walk?

(A) 6 blocks

(B) 15 blocks

(C) 21 blocks

(D) 16 blocks

(E) 25 blocks

20. In line 39, Jonah's uses the phrase "as the crow flies" to mean

(A) a scalar quantity

(B) a resultant vector

(C) a projectile motion

(D) a vertical component

(E) a horizontal component

Holt Physics: Two-Dimensional Motion and Vectors
Improving Sentences

DIRECTIONS: For each question in this section, select the best answer from among the choices given and fill in the corresponding circle on the answer sheet.

Part of each sentence in items 21 and 22 is underlined. Below each sentence are five ways of phrasing the underlined material. Choice A repeats the original phrasing; the other four choices are different. Choose the answer you think produces the most accurate sentence.

21. When you add vectors graphically, the resultant is the vector drawn <u>from the head of the first vector to the head of the last vector</u>.

    (A) from the head of the first vector to the head of the last vector

    (B) from the tail of the first vector to the head of the last vector

    (C) from the tail of the first vector to the tail of the last vector

    (D) from the head of the first vector to the tail of the last vector

    (E) between the midpoint of the two vectors

22. Two very different descriptions of an object's motion can still be correct <u>if the object does not change direction</u>.

    (A) if the object does not change direction

    (B) if the observers are in the same location

    (C) if the observers are in different locations

    (D) if they are measured from the exact frame of reference

    (E) if they are both described in relation to the center of Earth

Each sentence in items 23 and 24 contains either a single error or no error at all. If the sentence contains an error, choose the one underlined part that must be changed to make the sentence correct. If the sentence is correct, select choice E.

23. If you ignore <u>air resistance</u>, a <u>projectile</u> has
             A   B
    a constant <u>horizontal velocity</u> and a
             C
    constant <u>upward</u> acceleration. <u>No error</u>
          D   E

24. You can <u>resolve</u> a vector into its
           A
    <u>component</u> vectors by using the <u>sine</u> and
         B   C
    <u>cosine</u> functions. <u>No error</u>
         D   E

Holt Physics: Forces and the Laws of Motion
Essay

DIRECTIONS: The essay gives you an opportunity to show how effectively you can develop and express ideas. You should, therefore, take care to develop your ideas, present concepts logically and clearly, and use language precisely.

Your essay must be written on your own paper. You may use both sides of a single sheet of notebook paper. You will have enough space if you write on every line, avoid wide margins, and keep your handwriting to a reasonable size. Remember that people who are not familiar with your handwriting will read what you write. Try to write or print so that what you are writing is legible to those readers.

IMPORTANT REMINDERS:
- **A pencil is required for the essay.** An essay written in ink will receive a score of zero.
- **Do not write your essay in your test book.** You will receive credit only for what you write on a single sheet of notebook paper.
- **An off-topic essay will receive a score of zero.**

Think carefully about the concept presented in the following passage and the assignment below.

Several forces can act on a car at once. The resulting motion depends on the magnitude and direction of these forces. When they are all added together, the resultant is the net force acting on the car. For example, gravity causes the car to exert a downward force on the road. According to Newton's Third Law, if two objects interact, they exert equal and opposite forces on one another. In this case, the road exerts an upward force on the car equal to the downward pull of gravity. The diagram below shows two other forces acting on a car: the force of friction and the force generated by the motor.

ASSIGNMENT: Identify each force labeled in the diagram. In what direction does the net force acting on the car point? Which of Newton's laws predicts that this car will move in the direction of that net force? Plan and write an essay in which you address these questions. Support your explanation with reasoning and examples taken from your reading, studies, experience, or observations.

Holt Physics: Forces and the Laws of Motion
Mathematics

DIRECTIONS: In this section, solve each problem using any available space on the page for scratch work. Then decide which of the choices given is best and fill in the corresponding circle on the answer sheet.

NOTES:
1. The use of a calculator is permitted. All numbers used are real numbers.
2. Figures that accompany problems in this test are intended to provide information useful in solving the problems. They are drawn as accurately as possible EXCEPT when it is stated in a specific problem that the figure is not drawn to scale. All figures lie in a plane unless otherwise indicated.

<table>
<tr><td>Newton's Second Law

$\Sigma F = ma$</td><td>Coefficient of Static Friction

$\mu_s = \dfrac{F_{s,max}}{F_n}$</td></tr>
<tr><td>Coefficient of Kinetic Friction

$\mu_k = \dfrac{F_k}{F_n}$</td><td>Magnitude of the Force of Friction

$F_f = \mu F_n$</td></tr>
</table>

Reference Information

1. Two astronauts on a space walk push a tool case at the same time. One astronaut pushes the case with a force of 3.10 N away from the spacecraft. The second astronaut pushes the case with a force 1.80 N along the length of the spacecraft towards its rear. What is the magnitude and direction of the net force on the case?

 (A) 1.30 N away from the space ship

 (B) 3.10 N away from the space ship

 (C) 2.45 N at an angle 45° from the ship's rear

 (D) 4.90 N at an angle 45° from the ship's rear

 (E) 3.58 N at an angle 60° from the ship's rear

2. A motorboat's engine exerts a force of 360 N eastward on the boat. The water's current exerts a force of 270 N northward on the motorboat. What is the magnitude and direction of the net force on the motorboat?

 (A) 90 N to the northeast

 (B) 315 N to the northeast

 (C) 360 N to the east

 (D) 450 N at 37° north of east

 (E) 630 N at 37° north of east

GO ON TO THE NEXT PAGE

Mathematics *continued*

3. The net force on a 12 kg cart is 3.2 N backward. Ignoring friction, what is the acceleration of the cart?

   (A) 0.27 m/s² backward

   (B) 3.8 m/s² backward

   (C) 8.2 m/s² backward

   (D) 18 m/s² backward

   (E) 38 m/s² backward

4. A softball pitcher throws a softball with a force of 3.02 N, accelerating the ball at a rate of 15.9 m/s². What is the mass of the softball?

   (A) 0.0526 kg

   (B) 0.190 kg

   (C) 5.26 kg

   (D) 12.9 kg

   (E) 18.9 kg

5. An ice skater pushes against a wall with a force of 59 N. Ignoring friction, if the ice skater has a total mass of 79 kg, what is the magnitude of his acceleration?

   (A) 0.75 m/s²

   (B) 1.3 m/s²

   (C) 21 m/s²

   (D) 69 m/s²

   (E) 140 m/s²

6. A nurse pushes a woman in a wheelchair at a constant acceleration up a ramp for a period of 17.5 s. At the base of the ramp, the wheel chair is at rest, and at the top of the ramp, the wheelchair has a velocity of 0.50 m/s. The woman and her wheelchair have a combined mass of 65.0 kg. What is the magnitude of the net force on the woman and her wheelchair as they accelerate up the ramp?

   (A) 0.27 N

   (B) 1.9 N

   (C) 2.3 N

   (D) 3.7 N

   (E) 32 N

7. A robot that is exploring the surface of Mars has a mass of 136 kg. If the gravitational force acting on the robot is 504.6 N downward, what is the robot's free-fall acceleration?

   (A) 0.270 m/s² downward

   (B) 3.71 m/s² downward

   (C) 9.81 m/s² downward

   (D) 367 m/s² downward

   (E) 829 m/s² downward

8. A 35 kg wooden chest initially at rest on the wooden floor of a theater stage requires a 138 N horizontal force to set it in motion. What is the coefficient of static friction between the chest and the stage?

   (A) 0.21

   (B) 0.25

   (C) 0.40

   (D) 2.5

   (E) 3.9

GO ON TO THE NEX PAGE

| Mathematics *continued*

9. A waitress wants to slide a 1.89 kg pitcher of lemonade on a glass countertop. The coefficient of static friction between two glass objects is 0.900. What is the maximum value of the force of static friction for sliding the pitcher on the countertop?

   (A) 0.476 N

   (B) 1.70 N

   (C) 2.10 N

   (D) 16.7 N

   (E) 20.6 N

10. The coefficient of kinetic friction between a dresser and a wooden floor is 0.200. The dresser weighs 556 N. What is the force of kinetic friction that movers must overcome when sliding the dresser across the floor?

   (A) 11.3 N

   (B) 56.7 N

   (C) 111 N

   (D) 283 N

   (E) 2780 N

11. A 9.0 kg potted plant slides down a 25.0° incline with an acceleration of 2.4 m/s^2. What is the coefficient of kinetic friction between the potted plant and the incline?

   (A) 0.013

   (B) 0.012

   (C) 0.20

   (D) 0.24

   (E) 0.47

Question 12 is based on the following illustration of a 6.75 kg box on a ramp with a 30.0º incline.

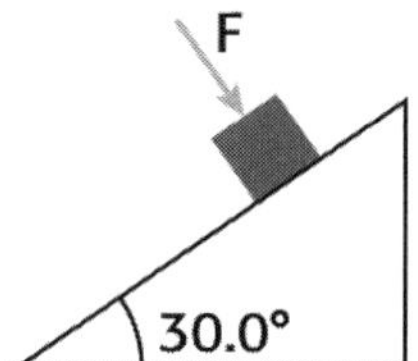

12. The coefficient of static friction between the box and the ramp is 0.500. What is the magnitude of the minimum force, *F*, that must be applied to the box perpendicularly to the ramp to prevent the box from sliding?

   (A) 16.6 N

   (B) 28.6 N

   (C) 90.4 N

   (D) 124 N

   (E) 168 N

Holt Physics: Forces and the Laws of Motion
Sentence Completion

DIRECTIONS: For each question in this section, select the best answer from among the choices given and fill in the corresponding circle on the answer sheet.

13. When forces on an object are unbalanced, the object experiences ______.

    (A) rest

    (B) free fall

    (C) an acceleration

    (D) a constant velocity

    (E) no change in motion

14. The tendency of a moving object to resist a change in speed or direction is called ______.

    (A) kinetic friction

    (B) inertia

    (C) mass

    (D) static friction

    (E) weight

15. According to Newton's Third Law, when two objects exert force on each other, the forces are equal in ______ and opposite in ______.

    (A) direction . . magnitude

    (B) magnitude . . direction

    (C) static friction . . kinetic friction

    (D) kinetic friction . . static friction

    (E) horizontal components . . vertical components

16. A(n) ______ force is a force that acts on an object in a direction perpendicular to the surface of contact.

    (A) air resistance

    (B) gravitational

    (C) kinetic friction

    (D) normal

    (E) static friction

Holt Physics: Forces and the Laws of Motion
Reading Passages

The passages below are followed by questions based on their content; questions following a pair of related passages may also be based on the relationship between the paired passages. Answer the questions on the basis of what is <u>stated</u> or <u>implied</u> in the passages. For each question in this section, select the best answer from the choices given and fill in the corresponding circle on the answer sheet.

Questions 17 and 18 are based on the following passage and diagram.

The Chungs live on a hill with a yard that slopes upward at a 5° angle. Every autumn, Mr. Chung uses a tarp to move
Line piles of raked leaves from the bottom
5 of the hill to the top of the hill, where he keeps a compost pile. Sometimes this process requires more effort than at other times. For example, if the leaves are wet and therefore have more mass, it takes a
10 greater force to drag them up the hill than when they are dry. When the wind is blowing in the same direction that Mr. Chung is moving the leaves, it takes less effort. On the other hand, when the wind
15 is blowing against him, it is more difficult.

Mr. Chung used to use a rough piece of burlap to move the leaves up the hill. However, he later found that a plastic tarp
20 created less friction with the ground than the burlap did. Because friction acts against movement, it took more effort for him to move the burlap than the plastic tarp with a similar mass of leaves.

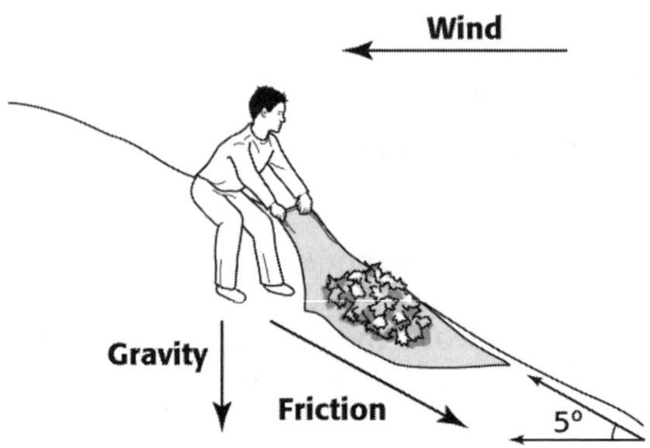

17. The word "effort" in line 7 refers to

   (A) mass

   (B) friction

   (C) a normal force

   (D) an applied force

   (E) acceleration due to gravity

18. Lines 17–24 suggest that using a plastic tarp rather than a piece of burlap

   (A) reduced friction between the leaves and the tarp

   (B) increased friction between the leaves and the tarp

   (C) reduced friction between the tarp and the ground

   (D) increased friction between the tarp and the ground

   (E) increased force associated with the acceleration due to gravity

GO ON TO THE NEXT PAGE

Reading Passages *continued*

Questions 19 and 20 are based on the following passage.

Quentin used a spring scale to explore the force of friction between a wooden block and a laboratory table. He

Line diagrammed each stage of his exploration.

5 When the block is resting on the table, as shown in Figure (A) below, Quentin inferred that the only forces that exist in the system are the force of gravity pulling the block towards the table and the

10 reaction force of the table holding up the block. Because these forces are equal and in exactly opposite directions, they cancel each other out, resulting in a net force of zero on the block.

15 When Quentin applied a small horizontal force to the side of the block, the block did not move. He inferred that the table exerted an equal force in the opposite direction, canceling his force.

20 This force is the force of static friction, shown in Figure (B) below, caused by the roughness of the surfaces of the two objects.

 However, when Quentin applied a

25 large enough horizontal force, the block moved in the direction of the force. His horizontal force overcame the force of

static friction, allowing him to move the block sideways. Quentin inferred that

30 friction still played a role in the system. He drew Figure (C) to illustrate how kinetic friction made the block more difficult to move than if the two objects were made of materials that produced

35 very little friction between them.

19. The term "system" in line 8 refers to

 (A) the spring scale and laboratory table

 (B) Quentin's hand and the wooden block

 (C) the spring scale and the wooden block

 (D) the wooden block and the laboratory table

 (E) the air and all of the physical objects in the room

20. Lines 31–35 imply that the kinetic friction between two objects

 (A) is a rare force

 (B) cannot be overcome

 (C) is not related to motion

 (D) depends on their materials

 (E) is greater than static friction

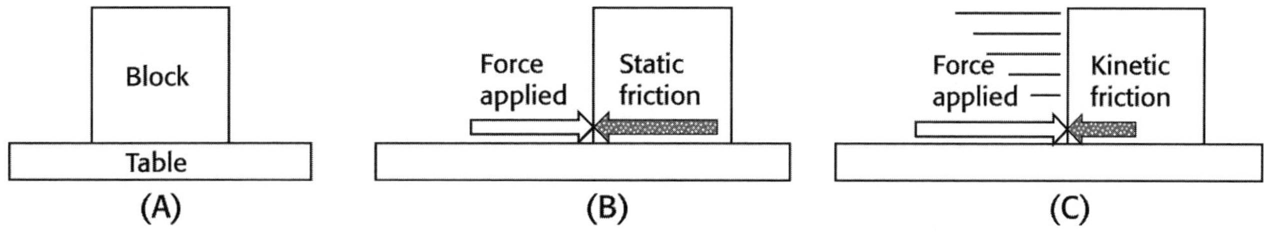

Holt Physics: Forces and the Laws of Motion
Improving Sentences

DIRECTIONS: For each question in this section, select the best answer from among the choices given and fill in the corresponding circle on the answer sheet.

Part of each sentence in items 21 and 22 is underlined. Below each sentence are five ways of phrasing the underlined material. Choice A repeats the original phrasing; the other four choices are different. Choose the answer you think produces the most accurate sentence.

21. An object in equilibrium is either at rest or moving with a constant acceleration.

    (A) moving with a constant acceleration

    (B) moving with a constant velocity

    (C) experiencing a positive net force

    (D) experiencing a negative net force

    (E) experiencing a changing net force

22. The force of friction between two surfaces is usually opposite the direction of the normal force.

    (A) usually opposite the direction of

    (B) proportional to

    (C) always greater than

    (D) equal in magnitude to

    (E) usually parallel to the direction of

Each sentence in items 23 and 24 contains either a single error or no error at all. If the sentence contains an error, choose the one underlined part that must be changed to make the sentence correct. If the sentence is correct, select choice E.

23. Newton's third law states that when the net
             A   B
    external force on an object is zero, the
                       C
    object's acceleration is zero. No error
           D   E

24. An object's weight, which is not dependent
               A   B
    on the object's location, is a measure of the
               C
    gravitational force exerted on the object.
            D
    No error
       E

Holt Physics: Work and Energy
Essay

DIRECTIONS: The essay gives you an opportunity to show how effectively you can develop and express ideas. You should, therefore, take care to develop your ideas, present concepts logically and clearly, and use language precisely.

Your essay must be written on your own paper. You may use both sides of a single sheet of notebook paper. You will have enough space if you write on every line, avoid wide margins, and keep your handwriting to a reasonable size. Remember that people who are not familiar with your handwriting will read what you write. Try to write or print so that what you are writing is legible to those readers.

IMPORTANT REMINDERS:
- **A pencil is required for the essay.** An essay written in ink will receive a score of zero.
- **Do not write your essay in your test book.** You will receive credit only for what you write on a single sheet of notebook paper.
- **An off-topic essay will receive a score of zero.**

Think carefully about the concept presented in the following passage and diagram and the assignment below.

The diagram below shows a roller coaster track. Points *A–E* indicate locations of the roller coaster car at different times as it travels along the track.

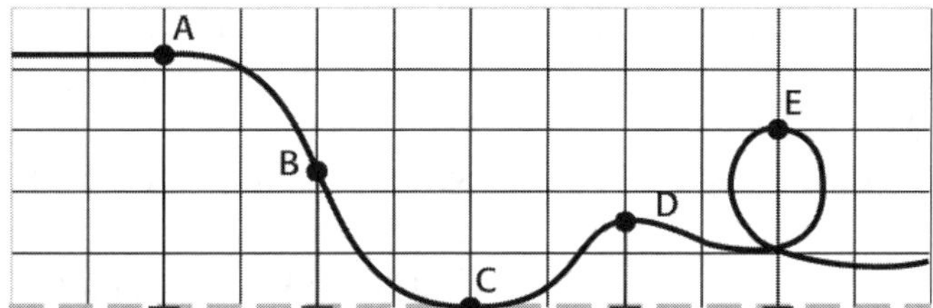

ASSIGNMENT: What are potential energy, kinetic energy, and mechanical energy? How does the car's potential and kinetic energy change as it rides along the track? Describe each quantity at each point. How do these quantities affect the car's mechanical energy at each point? Plan and write an essay in which you address these questions. Support your explanation with reasoning and examples taken from your reading, studies, experience, or observations.

Holt Physics: Work and Energy
Mathematics

DIRECTIONS: In this section, solve each problem using any available space on the page for scratch work. Then decide which of the choices given is best and fill in the corresponding circle on the answer sheet.

NOTES:
1. The use of a calculator is permitted. All numbers used are real numbers.
2. Figures that accompany problems in this test are intended to provide information useful in solving the problems. They are drawn as accurately as possible EXCEPT when it is stated in a specific problem that the figure is not drawn to scale. All figures lie in a plane unless otherwise indicated.

Reference Information

Net Work Done by Constant Net Force	**Kinetic Energy**
$W_{net} = F_{net}d \cos\theta$	$KE = \dfrac{1}{2}mv^2$
Work-Kinetic Energy Theorem	**Gravitational Potential Energy**
$W_{net} = \Delta KE$	$PE_g = mgh$
Elastic Potential Energy	**Conservation of Mechanical Energy**
$PE_{elastic} = \dfrac{1}{2}kx^2$	$ME_i = ME_f$
Power	$g = 9.81 \text{ m/s}^2$
$P = \dfrac{W}{\Delta t}$ or $P = Fv$	

1. What is the speed of a 1500 kg car if its kinetic energy is 4.7×10^5 J?

   (A) 18 m/s

   (B) 25 m/s

   (C) 63 m/s

   (D) 310 m/s

   (E) 630 m/s

2. When first hit, a golf ball has a kinetic energy of 96.5 J and travels at a speed of 65.0 m/s. What is its mass?

   (A) 1.72 g

   (B) 2.97 g

   (C) 5.71 g

   (D) 22.8 g

   (E) 45.7 g

GO ON TO THE NEXT PAGE

Mathematics *continued*

3. A child pulls a wagon with a constant force of 25.0 N at 35.0° from the horizontal and causes the wagon to move along a straight path for 15.0 m. How much work is done on the wagon?

   (A) 10.7 J

   (B) 307 J

   (C) 375 J

   (D) 476 J

   (E) 845 J

4. If 63 J of work is done in lifting a 6.8 kg bag of groceries, how far is it lifted?

   (A) 0.94 cm

   (B) 9.3 cm

   (C) 91 cm

   (D) 94 cm

   (E) 930 cm

5. A man has three friends help him push his dead car on a horizontal surface. The friends push with a constant total force of 1200 N. How far must the car be pushed, starting from rest, so that its final kinetic energy is 4200 J? (Disregard friction.)

   (A) 2.6 m

   (B) 3.5 m

   (C) 8.3 m

   (D) 11 m

   (E) 14 m

6. Two restaurant employees push a 730 kg wheeled dumpster along a horizontal surface. After they push the dumpster a distance of 5.5 m starting from rest, its speed is 0.75 m/s. What is the magnitude of the net force on the dumpster?

   (A) 3.8 N

   (B) 37 N

   (C) 210 N

   (D) 370 N

   (E) 1100 N

7. A toy spring with a spring constant of 6.4 N/m has a relaxed length of 20.0 cm. When a ball is attached to the end of the spring and allowed to come to rest, the vertical length of the spring is 75.0 cm. What is the elastic potential energy stored in the spring?

   (A) 0.97 J

   (B) 1.7 J

   (C) 3.5 J

   (D) 17 J

   (E) 9700 J

8. In a grandfather clock, a 455 g pendulum weight hangs on a rod that is 1.00 m long. What is the gravitational potential energy associated with the pendulum weight relative to its lowest position when the rod makes a 45.0° angle with the vertical?

   (A) 1.31 J

   (B) 2.23 J

   (C) 3.16 J

   (D) 4.46 J

   (E) 13.1 J

GO ON TO THE NEXT PAGE

Mathematics *continued*

9. A supply helicopter is flying over a remote military base when it drops a 45.0 kg package. If the altitude of the helicopter is 55 m and friction is disregarded, what is the speed of the package when it hits the ground?

   (A) 9.8 m/s

   (B) 11 m/s

   (C) 16 m/s

   (D) 23 m/s

   (E) 33 m/s

10. A tire swing is released from some initial height such that the speed of the tire at the bottom of the swing is 2.5 m/s. What is the initial height of the tire?

    (A) 0.13 m

    (B) 0.16 m

    (C) 0.32 m

    (D) 3.1 m

    (E) 31 m

11. A mover pushes a 245 kg piano so that it accelerates uniformly from rest to 1.5 m/s in 5.00 s. What is the power delivered by the mover in this time interval?

    (A) 55 W

    (B) 110 W

    (C) 280 W

    (D) 540 W

    (E) 3600 W

12. How long does it take a 15 kW car motor to do 4.7×10^6 J of work?

    (A) 0.32 s

    (B) 3.1 s

    (C) 71 s

    (D) 310 s

    (E) 71 000 s

Holt Physics: Work and Energy
Sentence Completion

**DIRECTIONS: For each question in this section, select the best answer from
among the choices given and fill in the corresponding circle on the answer sheet.**

13. When the force on an object and the
object's displacement are in different
directions, only the component of the force
that is _______ to the object's displacement
does work.

(A) horizontal

(B) normal

(C) parallel

(D) perpendicular

(E) vertical

14. The net work done on a body equals its
change in _______.

(A) mass

(B) position

(C) kinetic energy

(D) potential energy

(E) mechanical energy

15. _______ energy is the sum of the kinetic
energy and all forms of _______ energy.

(A) Potential . . mechanical

(B) Mechanical . . potential

(C) Potential . . elastic potential

(D) Potential . . gravitational potential

(E) Mechanical . . gravitational potential

16. _______ is a quantity that measures the rate
at which work is done or energy is
transformed.

(A) Work

(B) Power

(C) Kinetic energy

(D) Potential energy

(E) Mechanical energy

Holt Physics: Work and Energy
Reading Passage

The passages below are followed by questions based on their content; questions following a pair of related passages may also be based on the relationship between the paired passages. Answer the questions on the basis of what is <u>stated</u> or <u>implied</u> in the passages. For each question in this section, select the best answer from the choices given and fill in the corresponding circle on the answer sheet.

Questions 17–20 are based on the following passage.

A cyborg, as any science-fiction aficionado knows, is part human and part machine and is able to perform
Line extraordinary tasks. Although cyborgs are
5 still more fiction than science, Dr. Homayoon Kazerooni, of the University of California at Berkeley, has been inventing machines called human extenders that can give mere mortals
10 superhuman strength.

"Human extenders are robotic systems worn by a human to move heavy objects," Dr. Kazerooni says. One of the first machines Dr. Kazerooni designed is
15 a 1.5 m-long steel arm that weighs thousands of newtons (several hundred pounds) and is attached to a pedestal on the floor. The operator inserts one arm into the device, and an attached computer
20 senses the arm's movement and uses hydraulic pressure to move the extender in conjunction with the operator's arm. The extender allows the operator to perform the same amount of work by
25 exerting less force. For example, when operating the extender, a person can lift objects weighing as much as 890 N while exerting a force of only 89 N.

30 Dr. Kazerooni is developing a complete suit of human extenders that will be powered by electricity. Controlled completely by the movement of the user, the suit has two arms that sense and
35 respond to both the force applied by the human and the weight of the object being lifted, taking most of the effort away from the operator. The machine's legs are able to balance the weight of the equipment,
40 and they attach at the operator's feet to allow movement around the room.

Dr. Kazerooni envisions human extenders being used primarily as labor aids for factory workers. Approximately
45 30 percent of all workplace accidents in the United States are related to back injuries, and they are usually the result of repeated lifting and moving of heavy objects. Human extenders could solve that
50 problem. "The person who is wearing the machine," Dr. Kazerooni says, "will feel less force and less fatigue, and therefore the potential for back injuries or any kind of injury would be less."

GO ON TO THE NEXT PAGE

Reading Passage *continued*

17. According to lines 1–10,

    (A) cyborgs will always be fictional

    (B) cyborgs require more power than humans

    (C) humans can get strength from electrical treatments

    (D) surgically attaching machines will give humans new strength

    (E) an invention that gives humans new strength is like a fictional cyborg

18. In line 10, the phrase "superhuman strength" means

    (A) powers that come from magic

    (B) strength of an ordinary human

    (C) strength of a very strong human

    (D) power that comes from electricity

    (E) strength greater than a human's strength

19. According to lines 23–29, how does the work done on an object while the operator wears the extender compare to the work done by the operator without the extender?

    (A) They are the same.

    (B) The work done with the extender is less than the work done without it.

    (C) The work done with the extender is more than the work done without it.

    (D) The relative values of the work vary depending on the strength of the operator.

    (E) The relative values of the work vary depending on the load that is worked on.

20. Given the equation for work, what can you conclude about the force applied to the object and the distance that the object is moved when the extender is used?

    (A) The same force must be applied to the object to move the object the same distance while doing the same amount of work.

    (B) The distance must remain the same for the force to increase with the same amount of work.

    (C) The object must move a longer distance to undergo the same amount of work with less force.

    (D) The object must move a shorter distance to undergo the same amount of work with less force.

    (E) The distance must remain the same for the force to decrease with the same amount of work.

Holt Physics: Work and Energy
Improving Sentences

DIRECTIONS: For each question in this section, select the best answer from among the choices given and fill in the corresponding circle on the answer sheet.

Part of each sentence in items 21 and 22 is underlined. Below each sentence are five ways of phrasing the underlined material. Choice A repeats the original phrasing; the other four choices are different. Choose the answer you think produces the most accurate sentence.

21. When you hold a heavy backpack out at arms length, <u>no work is done on the backpack</u>.

    (A) no work is done on the backpack

    (B) the backpack's potential energy is zero

    (C) the work done on the backpack is related to its mass and height

    (D) the work done on the backpack is related to its mass and your arm's length

    (E) the backpack's potential energy is related to its mass and your arm's length

22. Compressing a spring <u>decreases its mechanical energy</u>.

    (A) decreases its mechanical energy

    (B) decreases its elastic potential energy

    (C) increases its elastic potential energy

    (D) decreases its gravitational potential energy

    (E) increases its gravitational potential energy

Each sentence in items 23 and 24 contains either a single error or no error at all. If the sentence contains an error, choose the one underlined part that must be changed to make the sentence correct. If the sentence is correct, select choice E.

23. In the <u>presence</u> of <u>friction</u>, the amount of
         A   B
    <u>mechanical</u> energy in a system remains
      C
    <u>constant</u>. <u>No error</u>
      D   E

24. Machines with <u>different</u> <u>power</u> ratings do
           A   B
    different amounts of <u>work</u> in the same
        C
    <u>time</u> interval. <u>No error</u>
      D   E

Holt Physics: Momentum and Collisions
Essay

DIRECTIONS: The essay gives you an opportunity to show how effectively you can develop and express ideas. You should, therefore, take care to develop your ideas, present concepts logically and clearly, and use language precisely.

Your essay must be written on your own paper. You may use both sides of a single sheet of notebook paper. You will have enough space if you write on every line, avoid wide margins, and keep your handwriting to a reasonable size. Remember that people who are not familiar with your handwriting will read what you write. Try to write or print so that what you are writing is legible to those readers.

IMPORTANT REMINDERS:
- **A pencil is required for the essay.** An essay written in ink will receive a score of zero.
- **Do not write your essay in your test book.** You will receive credit only for what you write on a single sheet of notebook paper.
- **An off-topic essay will receive a score of zero.**

Think carefully about the concept presented in the following passage and diagram and the assignment below.

Historically, when a cannon fired a cannon ball, operators had to take care to avoid injury due to recoil. Recoil is the backward force produced when the gunpowder explodes and projects the cannon ball out of the front end of the cannon's cylinder. Many cannons had wheels that allowed them to be positioned easily and also allowed them to roll backwards slightly when fired. A very heavy cannon could do quite a bit of damage to the toes of unwary operators.

ASSIGNMENT: How does conservation of momentum explain recoil? What effect does a gunpowder explosion inside the cannon have on a small cannon ball? How does this effect compare to that on the more massive cannon? Plan and write an essay in which you address these questions. Support your explanation with reasoning and examples taken from your reading, studies, experience, or observations.

Holt Physics: Momentum and Collisions
Mathematics

DIRECTIONS: In this section, solve each problem using any available space on the page for scratch work. Then decide which of the choices given is best and fill in the corresponding circle on the answer sheet.

NOTES:
1. The use of a calculator is permitted. All numbers used are real numbers.
2. Figures that accompany problems in this test are intended to provide information useful in solving the problems. They are drawn as accurately as possible EXCEPT when it is stated in a specific problem that the figure is not drawn to scale. All figures lie in a plane unless otherwise indicated.

<table>
<tr><td rowspan="5" style="writing-mode: vertical-rl;">Reference Information</td><td>

Momentum

$\mathbf{p} = m\mathbf{v}$

Conservation of Momentum

$m_1\mathbf{v}_{1,i} + m_2\mathbf{v}_{2,i} = m_1\mathbf{v}_{1,f} + m_2\mathbf{v}_{2,f}$

</td><td>

Impulse=Momentum Theorem

$\mathbf{F}\Delta t = \Delta\mathbf{p}$ or $\mathbf{F}\Delta t = \Delta\mathbf{p} = m\mathbf{v}_f - m\mathbf{v}_i$

Perfectly Inelastic Collision

$m_1\mathbf{v}_{1,i} + m_2\mathbf{v}_{2,i} = (m_1 + m_2)\mathbf{v}_f$

</td></tr>
</table>

1. A cart with a mass of 25.0 kg is rolling with a speed of 14 m/s. What is the magnitude of the momentum of the cart?

   (A) 1.8 kg•m/s

   (B) 11 kg•m/s

   (C) 39 kg•m/s

   (D) 350 kg•m/s

   (E) 4900 kg•m/s

2. What velocity must a 2.25 kg croquet mallet have in order to have the same momentum as a 1.25 kg ball that has a momentum of 6.25 kg•m/s to the west?

   (A) 1.79 m/s to the west

   (B) 1.47 m/s to the west

   (C) 2.78 m/s to the west

   (D) 5.00 m/s to the west

   (E) 6.25 m/s to the west

GO ON TO THE NEXT PAGE

3. A 150 g pinball rolls towards a spring-loaded launching rod with a velocity of 2.0 m/s to the west. The launching rod strikes the pinball and causes it to move in the opposite direction with a velocity of 10.0 m/s. What impulse was delivered to the pinball by the launcher?

(A) 0.75 kg•m/s to the east

(B) 1.2 kg•m/s to the east

(C) 1.8 kg•m/s to the east

(D) 3.0 kg•m/s to the east

(E) 1800 kg•m/s to the east

4. A 63.5 kg cyclist riding a 13.6 kg bicycle is traveling south at a velocity of 9.00 m/s. If the cyclist applies a 69.4 N braking force that slows the bicycle down uniformly, how long does it take the cyclist to come to a complete stop?

(A) 1.76 s

(B) 6.47 s

(C) 8.23 s

(D) 10.0 s

(E) 13.3 s

5. A 72.0 kg stuntman jumps from a moving car to a 2.50 kg skateboard at rest. If the velocity of the car is 35.0 m/s to the east when the stuntman jumps, what is the final velocity of the stuntman and the skateboard?

(A) 1.22 m/s to the east

(B) 33.8 m/s to the east

(C) 36.2 m/s to the east

(D) 1010 m/s to the east

(E) 1040 m/s to the east

6. A girl on a 15 kg raft initially at rest throws a 3.0 kg life preserver to the north. If the life preserver has a speed of 5.0 m/s relative to the water, and the girl and the raft move in the opposite direction at 0.27 m/s, find the girl's mass.

(A) 1.0 kg

(B) 38 kg

(C) 41 kg

(D) 56 kg

(E) 330 kg

7. A 1.5 kg rolling pin rolls along a countertop at 6.0 m/s. It collides with and sticks to a 200 g lump of dough. The doughy rolling pin continues along the countertop. What is the final speed of the doughy rolling pin?

(A) 0.045 m/s

(B) 5.3 m/s

(C) 6.8 m/s

(D) 6.9 m/s

(E) 45 m/s

8. During a performance, a circus clown tosses a 10.5 kg prop at his 86.2 kg clown partner, who is wearing roller skates. The partner, who was initially at rest, begins to move 2.0 m/s towards the crowd when he catches the prop. What is the velocity of the prop before the collision?

(A) 0.22 m/s towards the crowd

(B) 0.24 m/s towards the crowd

(C) 14 m/s towards the crowd

(D) 16 m/s towards the crowd

(E) 18 m/s towards the crowd

GO ON TO THE NEXT PAGE

Mathematics *continued*

9. A 135 kg bumper car sliding to the right at 2.0 m/s on a frictionless surface makes an elastic head-on collision with a 135 kg bumper car moving to the left at 1.5 m/s. After the collision, the first bumper car moves to the left at 1.5 m/s. What is the velocity of the second bumper car after the collision?

   (A) 0.50 m/s to the right

   (B) 0.75 m/s to the right

   (C) 1.5 m/s to the right

   (D) 2.0 m/s to the right

   (E) 3.5 m/s to the right

10. A 6.75 kg bowling ball rolling away from you at 2.5 m/s makes an elastic head-on collision with a 5.50 kg bowling ball rolling toward you at 3.0 m/s. After the collision, the first bowling ball moves back towards you at 4.8 m/s. Disregard any effects of friction. What is the velocity of the second bowling ball after the collision?

   (A) 2.0 m/s away from you

   (B) 2.9 m/s away from you

   (C) 4.7 m/s away from you

   (D) 6.0 m/s away from you

   (E) 12 m/s away from you

Holt Physics: Momentum and Collisions
Sentence Completion

DIRECTIONS: For each question in this section, select the best answer from among the choices given and fill in the corresponding circle on the answer sheet.

11. The product of a constant applied force and the time interval during which the force is applied is the ______ of the force for the time interval.

    (A) elasticity

    (B) impulse

    (C) mass

    (D) momentum

    (E) velocity

12. To find an object's mass, divide its ______ by its velocity.

    (A) elasticity

    (B) impulse

    (C) mass

    (D) momentum

    (E) acceleration

13. A collision in which two objects stick together after colliding is called ______.

    (A) elastic

    (B) impulsive

    (C) perfectly inelastic

    (D) non-conserved

    (E) plastic

14. Momentum is conserved but kinetic energy is not conserved in a perfectly ______ collision.

    (A) elastic

    (B) impulsive

    (C) inelastic

    (D) non-conserved

    (E) plastic

Holt Physics: Momentum and Collisions
Reading Passages

The passages below are followed by questions based on their content; questions following a pair of related passages may also be based on the relationship between the paired passages. Answer the questions on the basis of what is <u>stated</u> or <u>implied</u> in the passages. For each question in this section, select the best answer from the choices given and fill in the corresponding circle on the answer sheet.

Questions 15–16 are based on the following passage.

 Emmy Noether was a famous German mathematician born in 1882, at a time when universities in her country did not allow women to formally enroll. Despite
Line
5 that prohibition, Noether was able to sit in on classes. Finally, in 1904, the Friedrich Alexander University of Erlangen permitted women to matriculate. Noether immediately enrolled in mathematics,
10 receiving her doctorate in 1907.
 Noether quickly established herself as a brilliant thinker. When she died in 1935, Albert Einstein himself wrote her obituary in the New York Times. Einstein
15 and other 20th century physicists formulated laws and theories that relied heavily on Noether's theorem, which says that energy, momentum, and other physical quantities are conserved because
20 the laws of physics do not change over time.

15. In line 5, the word "prohibition" means

 (A) court order

 (B) forbidding act

 (C) feeling of reluctance

 (D) abstinence from alcohol

 (E) obstruction of a bodily process

16. In line 19, the word "conserved" means

 (A) stored

 (B) released

 (C) not wasted

 (D) made new again

 (E) neither created nor destroyed

Questions 17–19 are based on the following passage.

 A popular toy that many people keep on their office desks consists of five metal balls, each suspended by two strings from
Line
 a simple frame. When at rest, all five balls
5 hang from the same height off the desk in a straight line. They can swing as a group from side to side when the ball on one of the ends is pushed toward the other balls.
 However, an amusing trick occurs
10 when you pull one of the end balls outward. When the ball at one end is pulled away from the other four balls and let go, it swings back into place hitting the next ball in line. At the moment it hits
15 the next ball, the ball on the opposite end swings out, as if invisibly pulled outward. When this ball swings back and hits its neighbor, the original ball is pushed outward in the same way. This continues
20 until the system loses energy. All the while, the balls in the center do not move at all.

GO ON TO THE NEXT PAGE

Reading Passages *continued*

17. When the toy is manipulated as described in lines 11–16, how does the momentum of the ball at one end compare to the momentum of the ball at the other end?

    (A) They are of equal magnitude and in the same direction.

    (B) They are of equal magnitude and in the opposite direction.

    (C) The ball at the closer end has a much greater momentum than the ball at the other end.

    (D) The ball at the closer end has a much smaller momentum than the ball at the other end.

    (E) The momentum of the ball at the closer end is unrelated to the momentum of the ball at the other end.

18. What physics concept explains this behavior?

    (A) Newton's first law

    (B) perfectly inelastic collision

    (C) conservation of momentum

    (D) impulse-momentum theorem

    (E) kinetic energy of a pendulum

19. How do the relative masses of the balls affect the way this toy works?

    (A) The masses of the balls must be equal for the velocities of the balls to be equal.

    (B) The first ball must have a greater mass than the last ball for the velocities of the balls to be equal.

    (C) The first ball must have a smaller mass than the last ball for the velocities of the balls to be equal.

    (D) The balls in the middle must have significantly smaller masses than the balls on the ends for the momentum to be transferred.

    (E) The balls in the middle must have significantly larger masses than the balls on the ends for the momentum to be transferred.

Holt Physics: Momentum and Collisions
Improving Sentences

DIRECTIONS: For each question in this section, select the best answer from among the choices given and fill in the corresponding circle on the answer sheet.

Part of each sentence in items 20–22 is underlined. Below each sentence are five ways of phrasing the underlined material. Choice A repeats the original phrasing; the other four choices are different. Choose the answer you think produces the most accurate sentence.

20. If a collision is perfectly elastic, the value of the total kinetic energy after the collision is equal to <u>zero</u>.

   (A) zero

   (B) one

   (C) half the total initial value

   (D) twice the total initial value

   (E) the value before the collision

21. When two objects push away from each other and their momentum is equal but opposite, the total momentum is <u>one</u>.

   (A) one

   (B) zero

   (C) less than the initial momentum

   (D) greater than the initial momentum

   (E) equal to twice that of one object

22. When two objects interact, the change in momentum of the first object is _______ the change in momentum of the second object.

   (A) equal to and opposite

   (B) less than and opposite

   (C) greater than and opposite

   (D) less than and in the same direction

   (E) greater than and in the same direction

Each sentence in items 23 and 24 contains either a single error or no error at all. If the sentence contains an error, choose the one underlined part that must be changed to make the sentence correct. If the sentence is correct, select choice E.

23. <u>Force</u> is <u>increased</u> when the <u>time interval</u>
     A   B   C
   of an <u>impact</u> is increased. <u>No error</u>
        D   E

24. In an <u>inelastic</u> collision, <u>momentum</u> can be
          A   B
   converted to internal elastic potential

   energy, <u>sound energy</u>, and <u>internal energy</u>.
            C   D
   <u>No error</u>
    E

Holt Physics: Circular Motion and Gravitation
Essay

DIRECTIONS: The essay gives you an opportunity to show how effectively you can develop and express ideas. You should, therefore, take care to develop your ideas, present concepts logically and clearly, and use language precisely.

Your essay must be written on your own paper. You may use both sides of a single sheet of notebook paper. You will have enough space if you write on every line, avoid wide margins, and keep your handwriting to a reasonable size. Remember that people who are not familiar with your handwriting will read what you write. Try to write or print so that what you are writing is legible to those readers.

IMPORTANT REMINDERS:
- **A pencil is required for the essay.** An essay written in ink will receive a score of zero.
- **Do not write your essay in your test book.** You will receive credit only for what you write on a single a sheet of notebook paper.
- **An off-topic essay will receive a score of zero.**

Think carefully about the concept presented in the following passage and the assignment below.

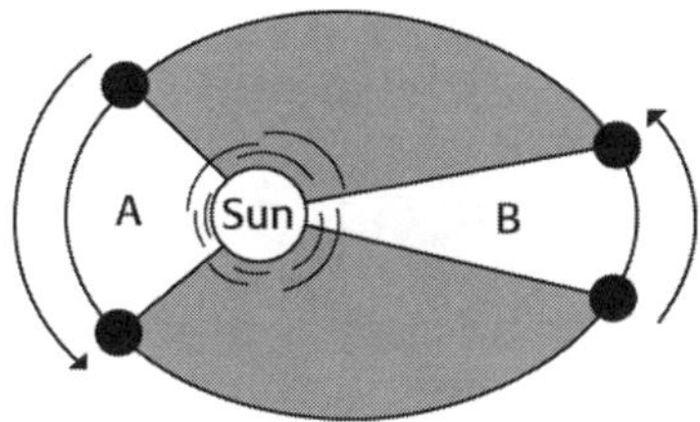

Johannes Kepler used the detailed observations of astronomer Tycho Brahe to refine the Copernican model, which described the planets moving around the sun in circular orbits. Kepler summarized his results in three scientific laws that explain how planets move. Kepler's First Law states that a planet has an elliptical orbit around the sun. According to Kepler's Second Law, illustrated in the image above, the imaginary line joining the sun and the planet sweeps out equal areas in equal time intervals. Kepler's Third Law states that the period of revolution for a planet orbiting the sun increases rapidly with the mean radius of its orbit.

ASSIGNMENT: What do Kepler's laws tell you about the distance between a planet and the sun? What do they tell you about the relative speed of a planet as it moves in its orbit? Plan and write an essay in which you address these questions. Support your explanation with reasoning and examples taken from your reading, studies, experience, or observations.

Holt Physics: Circular Motion and Gravitation
Mathematics

DIRECTIONS: In this section, solve each problem using any available space on the page for scratch work. Then decide which of the choices given is best and fill in the corresponding oval on the answer sheet.

NOTES:
1. The use of a calculator is permitted. All numbers used are real numbers.
2. Figures that accompany problems in this test are intended to provide information useful in solving the problems. They are drawn as accurately as possible EXCEPT when it is stated in a specific problem that the figure is not drawn to scale. All figures lie in a plane unless otherwise indicated.

Reference Information

Centripetal Acceleration

$$a_c = \frac{v_t^2}{r}$$

Centripetal Force

$$F_c = \frac{mv_t^2}{r}$$

Newton's Law of Universal Gravitation

$$F_g = G\frac{m_1 m_2}{r^2}, \; G = 6.673 \times 10^{-11} \; \frac{\text{N} \bullet \text{m}^2}{\text{kg}^2}$$

Torque

$$\tau = Fd \sin \theta$$

Period of an Object in Circular Orbit

$$T = 2\pi\sqrt{\frac{r^3}{Gm}}$$

Speed of an Object in Circular Orbit

$$v_t = \sqrt{G\frac{m}{r}}$$

Mechanical Advantage

$$MA = \frac{F_{out}}{F_{in}} = \frac{d_{in}}{d_{out}}$$

Efficiency of a Machine

$$eff = \frac{W_{out}}{W_{in}}$$

1. A pickle sits 8.0 cm from the center of a circular, rotating platter. The platter rotates such that the pickle's tangential speed is 4.8 cm/s. What is the pickle's centripetal acceleration?

   (A) 0.36 cm/s^2

   (B) 0.60 cm/s^2

   (C) 1.2 cm/s^2

   (D) 2.9 cm/s^2

   (E) 5.8 cm/s^2

2. A tether ball tied to a pole by a rope swings in a circular path with a centripetal acceleration of 2.7 m/s^2. If the ball has a tangential speed of 2.0 m/s, what is the diameter of the circular path in which it travels?

   (A) 0.74 m

   (B) 1.5 m

   (C) 3.0 m

   (D) 3.6 m

   (E) 7.3 m

GO ON TO THE NEXT PAGE

Mathematics *continued*

3. An inline skater skates on a circular track 120.0 m in diameter at a tangential speed of 9.20 m/s. If the skater's mass is 68.5 kg, what is the magnitude of the centripetal force on the skater?

   (A) 5.25 N

   (B) 10.5 N

   (C) 48.3 N

   (D) 96.6 N

   (E) 719 N

4. A man swings a bucket on a 120-cm rope with a tangential speed of 4.5 m/s. If the magnitude of the centripetal force is 25 N, what is the bucket's mass?

   (A) 1.5 kg

   (B) 2.6 kg

   (C) 6.7 kg

   (D) 74 kg

   (E) 300 kg

5. The planet Venus has a mass of 4.87×10^{24} kg and a radius of 6.05×10^{6} km. What is the magnitude of the gravitational force that an 81-kg person would experience while standing on the surface of Venus?

   (A) 179 N

   (B) 719 N

   (C) 259 N

   (D) 7.19×10^{8} N

   (E) 4.19×10^{9} N

6. The planet Venus has a mass of 4.87×10^{24} kg, and Earth has a mass of 5.97×10^{24} kg. How far apart are the two planets when they exert a gravitational force of 1.12×10^{18} N on one another?

   (A) 1.54×10^{3} m

   (B) 4.16×10^{10} m

   (C) 1.72×10^{21} m

   (D) 4.66×10^{28} m

   (E) 2.60×10^{31} m

7. What is the magnitude of the torque produced by a 2.0 N force applied to a bottle opener at a perpendicular distance 8.0 cm from the bottle top?

   (A) 0.11 N•m

   (B) 0.16 N•m

   (C) 0.28 N•m

   (D) 11 N•m

   (E) 16 N•m

8. If the torque needed to pry open a crate has a magnitude of 32.8 N•m, what is the minimum force that must be exerted at the end of a 0.900 m crowbar to open the crate?

   (A) 0.488 N

   (B) 0.602 N

   (C) 29.5 N

   (D) 36.4 N

   (E) 2090 N

GO ON TO THE NEXT PAGE

Mathematics *continued*

Questions 9 and 10 are based on the following illustration of the moon's orbit around Earth. The moon has a mass of 7.35 $\times 10^{22}$ kg, while the Earth has a mass of 5.97 $\times 10^{24}$ kg. NOTE: The figure is not to scale.

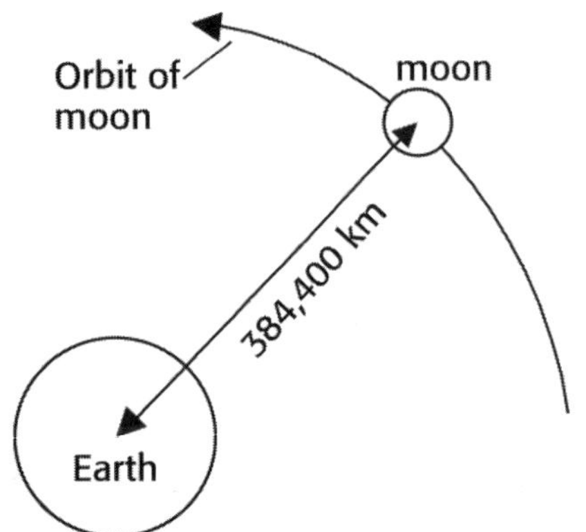

9. If the moon's orbit were circular according to the illustration above, what would be its period?

    (A) 9.00×10^2 s

    (B) 2.38×10^6 s

    (C) 2.14×10^7 s

    (D) 2.26×10^7 s

    (E) 1.42×10^8 s

10. If the moon's orbit were circular according to the illustration above, what would be its orbital speed?

    (A) 1.13×10^2 m/s

    (B) 1.02×10^3 m/s

    (C) 3.21×10^4 m/s

    (D) 3.56×10^4 m/s

    (E) 1.03×10^6 m/s

11. A person lifts a 500.0 N crate using a pulley system. If the person exerts a 125 N force to lift the crate, what is the mechanical advantage of the pulley system?

    (A) 1.25

    (B) 2.50

    (C) 3.75

    (D) 4.00

    (E) 5.00

12. The efficiency of a machine is 88 percent. How much work input is required to perform a work output of 45 J using the machine?

    (A) 2.0 J

    (B) 40 J

    (C) 43 J

    (D) 51 J

    (E) 200 J

GO ON TO THE NEXT PAGE

Holt Physics: Circular Motion and Gravitation
Sentence Completion

DIRECTIONS: For each question in this section, select the best answer from among the choices given and fill in the corresponding circle on the answer sheet.

13. A cart that is moving at a constant speed in a circle has a ______ acceleration and a ______ acceleration toward the center of zero.

    (A) zero directional . . centripetal

    (B) positive centripetal . . tangential

    (C) positive tangential . . centripetal

    (D) negative centripetal . . tangential

    (E) negative tangential . . centripetal

14. The gravitational force between two objects depends on mass and ______.

    (A) acceleration

    (B) density

    (C) distance

    (D) speed

    (E) volume

15. According to Kepler's First Law, the planets travel in ______ orbits around the sun.

    (A) circular

    (B) concentric

    (C) elliptical

    (D) horizontal

    (E) vertical

16. In physics, the ability of a force to rotate an object around some axis is measured by a quantity called ______.

    (A) centripetal acceleration

    (B) gravitational force

    (C) mechanical advantage

    (D) mechanical efficiency

    (E) torque

Holt Physics: Circular Motion and Gravitation
Reading Passages

The passages below are followed by questions based on their content. Answer the questions on the basis of what is <u>stated</u> or <u>implied</u> in the passages.

Questions 17 and 18 are based on the following passage.

Isaac Newton's law of universal gravitation answered two of the most puzzling questions in the history of
Line science: "Why does an object thrown into
5 the air fall back toward Earth?" and "What keeps the planets moving in the sky?" Newton said that all objects in the universe attract each other through the force of gravity. The same force that
10 causes objects to fall to Earth controls the motion of planets. Gravity affects all matter, with large masses exerting a stronger gravitational force than small masses. However, Newton's law of
15 gravity left several questions unanswered that continued to trouble scientists, including a strange "wobble" in the orbit of planet Mercury around the sun. Albert Einstein later answered those questions
20 with a theory that is now universally considered a law of nature: the General Theory of Relativity.

Imagine placing a tennis ball, baseball, basketball, and a table-tennis
25 ball around the perimeter of a large rubber sheet or a trampoline. Pretend that these balls model the solar system. Now, place a heavy bowling ball into the center of the rubber sheet or trampoline. What
30 happens? The rubber sheet or trampoline curves inward, dragging the lighter balls toward the bowling ball.

Einstein likened gravity to the actual curvature of the trampoline or rubber
35 sheet. He said that space and time together form a kind of flexible universal fabric that surrounds us and permeates the entire universe. Through gravity, a heavy mass curves the fabric of space and time
40 around itself, just like a heavy ball curves a rubber sheet toward itself.

17. According to lines 11–14, when all other factors are the same, as mass increases,

   (A) "wobble" increases

   (B) "wobble" decreases

   (C) "wobble" remains constant

   (D) gravitational force increases

   (E) gravitational force decreases

18. The model described in lines 23–41 of the passage compares gravity to

   (A) space and time

   (B) the fabric of the universe

   (C) the shape of a bowling ball

   (D) the curvature of a trampoline

   (E) the movement of lighter balls

GO ON TO THE NEXT PAGE

Reading Passage *continued*

Questions 19 and 20 are based on the following passage.

Astronomers have concluded that our solar system formed from a swirling cloud of gas and dust about 4.6 billion
Line years ago. The swirling cloud flattened to
5 become a disk. The sun formed at the center, and the planets formed from the same disk, but at different distances from the Sun.

Astronomers are less certain about
10 how the moon formed around the Earth. They know that the moon is made of material similar to the Earth's upper mantle, but the moon does not contain iron or other materials contained in the
15 Earth. They also know that the moon is round and orbits in the same direction and on the same plane as Earth, the ecliptic plane. Three astronomers share their opinions on the origin of the moon:

20 **Astronomer 1**
The moon formed out of Earth's crust and mantle. I call this theory the *collisional-ejection theory*. After Earth formed, a huge object that could have been the size
25 of the planet Mars crashed into Earth's surface. The energy from the impact tipped Earth on its axis and sent streams of vaporized material into space. The vaporized material formed a ring around
30 the planet near the ecliptic plane, and eventually came together to form the moon.

Astronomer 2
The moon formed when Earth's gravity
35 captured a large asteroid that passed nearby. This *capture theory* seems

logical, because other moons around other planets formed this way. We know, for instance, that Phobos and Deimos, two
40 moons of Mars, were passing asteroids captured by the gravitational force of Mars.

Astronomer 3
Both Earth and the moon formed together
45 at about the same time from the original disk-shaped cloud of gas and dust that formed the solar system. This *co-formation theory* says they formed very close to one another, which explains the
50 location of the moon relative to Earth and why the moon is rocky, rather than icy or gaseous.

19. Lines 15–18 suggest that the elliptical orbits of the moon and Earth

  (A) cover the same area

  (B) lie on the same plane

  (C) have similar perimeters

  (D) have the same average radius

  (E) are perpendicular to one another

20. The word "captured" in line 35 most likely means

  (A) pulled into orbit

  (B) took an image of

  (C) held the attention of

  (D) confined in a container

  (E) caused to erode over time

Holt Physics: Circular Motion and Gravitation
Improving Sentences

DIRECTIONS: For each question in this section, select the best answer from among the choices given and fill in the corresponding circle on the answer sheet.

Part of each sentence in items 21 and 22 is underlined. Below each sentence are five ways of phrasing the underlined material. Choice A repeats the original phrasing; the other four choices are different. Choose the answer you think produces the most accurate sentence.

21. An object in circular motion has a centripetal acceleration directed <u>outward from the center of</u> the circular path.

   (A) outward from the center of

   (B) parallel along

   (C) tangentially from

   (D) toward the center of

   (E) in a direction opposite from

22. When calculating gravitational force between two spherical objects, r is <u>the distance between their centers</u>.

   (A) the distance between their centers

   (B) the larger of the two radii

   (C) the smaller of the two radii

   (D) the average of their radii

   (E) the distance between their surfaces

Each sentence in items 23 and 24 contains either a single error or no error at all. If the sentence contains an error, choose the one underlined part that must be changed to make the sentence correct. If the sentence is correct, select choice E.

23. <u>Torque</u> depends how much <u>force</u> is
    A   B
applied to the <u>axis of rotation</u> and
            C
where the force is applied <u>along</u> the
                  D
lever arm. <u>No error</u>
        E

24. Because all real machines experience some

friction, the <u>efficiency</u> of a real
    A   B
machine is <u>always</u> <u>greater</u> than
         C   D
one. <u>No error</u>
    E

Holt Physics: Fluid Mechanics
Essay

DIRECTIONS: The essay gives you an opportunity to show how effectively you can develop and express ideas. You should, therefore, take care to develop your ideas, present concepts logically and clearly, and use language precisely.

Your essay must be written on your own paper. You may use both sides of a single sheet of notebook paper. You will have enough space if you write on every line, avoid wide margins, and keep your handwriting to a reasonable size. Remember that people who are not familiar with your handwriting will read what you write. Try to write or print so that what you are writing is legible to those readers.

IMPORTANT REMINDERS:
- **A pencil is required for the essay.** An essay written in ink will receive a score of zero.
- **Do not write your essay in your test book.** You will receive credit only for what you write on a single sheet of notebook paper.
- **An off-topic essay will receive a score of zero.**

Think carefully about the concept presented in the following passage and diagram and the assignment below.

The diagram below shows a cross-section view of an airplane wing and the flow of layers of air around the wing. The shape and position of the wing play important roles in flight. Wings are designed so that pilots can control how they interact with the surrounding fluid to raise a plane in the air and allow it to land safely.

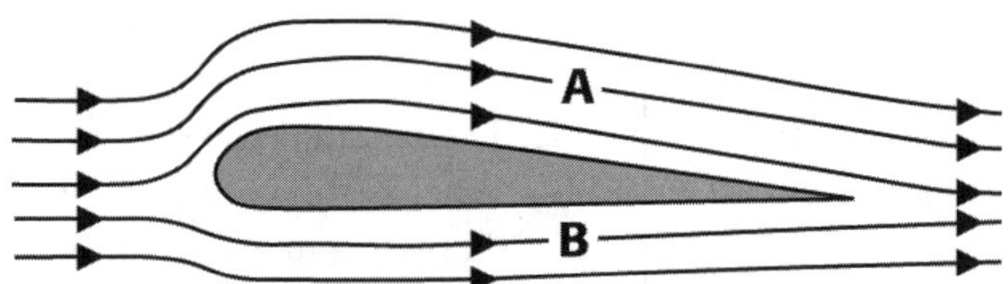

ASSIGNMENT: What is lift? What principle of fluid mechanics contributes to how airplanes achieve lift? How does fluid flow differ on either side of the airplane wing shown above? How does this difference lead to lift? Plan and write an essay in which you address these questions. Support your explanation with reasoning and examples taken from your reading, studies, experience, or observations.

Holt Physics: Fluid Mechanics
Mathematics

DIRECTIONS: In this section, solve each problem using any available space on the page for scratch work. Then decide which of the choices given is best and fill in the corresponding circle on the answer sheet.

NOTES:
1. The use of a calculator is permitted. All numbers used are real numbers.
2. Figures that accompany problems in this test are intended to provide information useful in solving the problems. They are drawn as accurately as possible EXCEPT when it is stated in a specific problem that the figure is not drawn to scale. All figures lie in a plane unless otherwise indicated.

<table>
<tr><td>

Reference Information

Mass Density

$$\rho = \frac{m}{V}$$

Buoyant Force

$$F_B = F_{g(displaced\ fluid)} = m_f g$$

Buoyant Force on Floating Objects

$$F_B = F_{g(object)} = m_o g$$

Atmospheric Pressure at Sea Level

$1\ atm = 1.01 \times 10^5\ Pa$

Density of Water

$\rho_{water} = 1.00 \times 10^3\ kg/m^3$

</td><td>

Pressure

$$P = \frac{F}{A}$$

Fluid Pressure as a Function of Depth

$$P = P_0 + \rho g h$$

Continuity Equation

$$A_1 v_1 = A_2 v_2$$

Area of a Circle

$$A = \pi r^2$$

</td></tr>
</table>

1. What is the density, expressed in kg/m^3, of a solid that has a mass of 393 g and a volume of $50.0\ cm^3$?

 (A) $1.27 \times 10^{-1}\ kg/m^3$

 (B) $7.86 \times 10^0\ kg/m^3$

 (C) $1.27 \times 10^2\ kg/m^3$

 (D) $3.43 \times 10^2\ kg/m^3$

 (E) $7.86 \times 10^3\ kg/m^3$

2. The density of ice is $9.17 \times 10^2\ kg/m^3$. What is the volume of a solid ice sculpture that has a mass of 1550 kg?

 (A) $0.592\ m^3$

 (B) $1.69\ m^3$

 (C) $633\ m^3$

 (D) $1550\ m^3$

 (E) $2470\ m^3$

GO ON TO THE NEXT PAGE

Mathematics *continued*

3. An aluminum machine part weighs 220.0 N in air and 138.6 N in water. What is the density of the aluminum part?

   (A) 3.70×10^2 kg/m^3

   (B) 6.30×10^2 kg/m^3

   (C) 1.59×10^3 kg/m^3

   (D) 2.70×10^3 kg/m^3

   (E) 2.65×10^4 kg/m^3

4. A raft is 1.5 m wide and 3.5 m long. When a crate is placed on the raft, it sinks 2.50 cm in the water. What is the weight of the crate?

   (A) 1.53×10^{-1} N

   (B) 1.33×10^0 N

   (C) 1.31×10^2 N

   (D) 1.29×10^3 N

   (E) 1.31×10^4 N

5. An oak log has a mass of 65.5 kg and a density of 695 kg/m^3. What is the magnitude of the buoyant force acting on the log when it is floating in water?

   (A) 45.5 N

   (B) 447 N

   (C) 643 N

   (D) 925 N

   (E) 2990 N

6. A woman's footprint has an area of 190 cm^2. If she has a mass of 67.8 kg, what pressure does she exert on the ground when standing on one foot?

   (A) 3.6×10^{-1} Pa

   (B) 7.0×10^0 Pa

   (C) 1.8×10^4 Pa

   (D) 3.5×10^4 Pa

   (E) 7.0×10^4 Pa

7. An antique table weighs 890 N. What total pressure does the table exert on the floor via four legs, each with a bottom surface that is 4 cm^2?

   (A) 5.7×10^4 Pa

   (B) 1.4×10^5 Pa

   (C) 2.3×10^5 Pa

   (D) 5.6×10^5 Pa

   (E) 2.2×10^6 Pa

8. In a pneumatic lift, compressed air exerts a force on a piston with a radius of 10.00 cm. This pressure is transmitted to a second piston with a radius of 25.0 cm. This second piston lifts a crate. Ignoring the weight of the pistons, how large a force must the compressed air exert to lift a crate that is 66.5 N?

   (A) 3.76 N

   (B) 26.6 N

   (C) 39.9 N

   (D) 99.8 N

   (E) 166 N

GO ON TO THE NEXT PAGE

Mathematics *continued*

9. A scuba diver dives to a depth of 15 m in a lake of water that has a density of 1.00×10^3 kg/m^3. How many times greater is the pressure at this depth than the pressure at the surface?

   (A) 0.41

   (B) 1.5

   (C) 2.5

   (D) 15

   (E) 41

10. A seismologist studying the sea floor designs an instrument case to be able to withstand pressure at a depth of 4.000×10^3 m. Sea water has a density of 1.025×10^3 kg/m^3. How much pressure, in Pa, must the case be able to withstand in order to protect the instruments it holds?

    (A) 4.10×10^6 Pa

    (B) 4.20×10^6 Pa

    (C) 4.02×10^7 Pa

    (D) 4.03×10^7 Pa

    (E) 4.04×10^8 Pa

11. A 2.5 cm diameter hose fills a 3.0×10^{-3} m^3 watering can in 5.0 s. What is the speed at which the water leaves the hose?

    (A) 0.069 m/s

    (B) 0.10 m/s

    (C) 0.31 m/s

    (D) 1.2 m/s

    (E) 33 m/s

Question 12 is based on the following illustration of a factory pipe system, which has a narrow section of pipe (3.5 cm in diameter) and a wide section of pipe (7.0 cm in diameter).

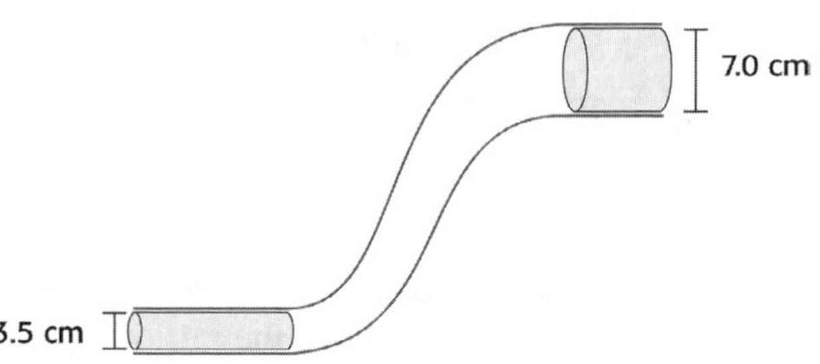

12. Water at a pressure of 9.00×10^5 Pa flows through the narrow section of the pipe system shown above at a speed of 5.00 m/s. What is the speed of the flow in the wider section of the pipe system?

    (A) 1.25 m/s

    (B) 1.80 m/s

    (C) 2.50 m/s

    (D) 4.00 m/s

    (E) 5.00 m/s

Holt Physics: Fluid Mechanics
Sentence Completion

DIRECTIONS: For each question in this section, select the best answer from among the choices given and fill in the corresponding circle on the answer sheet.

13. All ______, when poured from a smaller container to a larger one, spread out to fill the entire container.

    (A) fluids

    (B) gases

    (C) liquids

    (D) masses

    (E) solids

14. For an object floating in water, the buoyant force equals the object's ______.

    (A) density

    (B) mass

    (C) pressure

    (D) weight in air

    (E) weight when submerged underwater

15. As ______ increases within a fluid, pressure ______.

    (A) buoyancy . . decreases

    (B) density . . decreases

    (C) depth . . decreases

    (D) depth . . increases

    (E) speed . . increases

16. According to ______, the pressure in a fluid decreases as the fluid's velocity increases.

    (A) Archimedes' principle

    (B) Bernoulli's principle

    (C) the continuity equation

    (D) the definition of density

    (E) Pascal's principle

Holt Physics: Fluid Mechanics
Reading Passages

The passages below are followed by questions based on their content; questions following a pair of related passages may also be based on the relationship between the paired passages. Answer the questions on the basis of what is <u>stated</u> or <u>implied</u> in the passages. For each question in this section, select the best answer from the choices given and fill in the corresponding circle on the answer sheet.

Questions 17–20 are based on the following passages.

Passage 1

"Eureka! Eureka!"

Legend has it that the Greek mathematician Archimedes was taking a bath when he discovered his famous principle of buoyancy. He was so excited that he jumped out of the bath, forgot to dress, and ran through the streets shouting "Eureka!" which means, "I have found it!"

Archimedes' principle states that any object completely or partially submerged in a fluid experiences an upward buoyant force equal in magnitude to the weight of the fluid displaced by the object. This means that a fluid (such as air or water) can exert a force that buoys up a body immersed in the fluid. It explains how ships float and how helium balloons rise. A body less dense—with less mass per unit volume—than the fluid it is immersed in will float or rise. If the body is denser than the fluid, it will sink. Hot air is less dense than cool air, so hot-air balloons fly.

Another legend says Archimedes uncovered a fraud using his principle. King Hieron II of Syracuse suspected that his supposedly solid gold crown was actually partly made of silver.

Archimedes compared equal weights of gold and silver immersed in water. Then he immersed a gold crown and pure silver crown of identical size to compare their weights. These comparisons proved that the crown was not solid gold.

Passage 2

To apply Archimedes' Principle, the shape and position of a body must be taken into account. For example, the density of steel is greater than the density of water. However, a boat will float in water because its overall shape includes large regions of air that also displace water. This extra displacement contributes to the buoyant force on the boat. If a boat is placed on the water with one end lower than the water's surface, these regions of air can fill with water and the boat will sink.

17. According to lines 10–24 of Passage 1, helium

   (A) is not a fluid

   (B) defies gravity

   (C) floats in all fluids

   (D) is less dense than air

   (E) sinks in a fluid that is less dense

GO ON TO THE NEXT PAGE

18. What does Passage 1 imply that Archimedes discovered while in the bath?

    (A) Most crowns are not made of solid gold.

    (B) Soaps that float are filled with tiny air bubbles.

    (C) A boat will sink if it is placed upside down in the water.

    (D) The pressure of bath water decreases as its velocity increases.

    (E) Bath water exerts an upward buoyant force on a bather's body.

19. According to Passage 2, what characteristics other than material density determine whether an object will float in water?

    (A) color and texture

    (B) mass and volume

    (C) position and shape

    (D) pressure and velocity

    (E) temperature and time

20. According to the two passages, boats must be made out of materials that are

    (A) denser than water

    (B) less dense than water

    (C) similar to air in the way they react to water

    (D) shaped to displace enough fluid to overcome their weight

    (E) able to fill with water when the boat is positioned with one end lower than the water's surface

Holt Physics: Fluid Mechanics
Improving Sentences

DIRECTIONS: For each question in this section, select the best answer from among the choices given and fill in the corresponding circle on the answer sheet.

Part of each sentence in items 21 and 22 is underlined. Below each sentence are five ways of phrasing the underlined material. Choice A repeats the original phrasing; the other four choices are different. Choose the answer you think produces the most accurate sentence.

21. Liquids and gases are fluids, but liquids have a definite volume, <u>as do gases</u>.

   (A) as do gases

   (B) while gases do not

   (C) while gases cannot flow

   (D) while gases have a definite shape

   (E) while gases have atoms that are fixed in place

22. According to Pascal's principle, pressure applied to a fluid in a closed container is <u>related to the speed of the fluid in that container</u>.

   (A) related to the speed of the fluid in that container

   (B) transmitted equally to every point of the fluid

   (C) always equal to the pressure outside of the container

   (D) inversely related to the dimensions of each part of the container

   (E) directly proportional to the dimensions of each part of the container

Each sentence in items 23 and 24 contains either a single error or no error at all. If the sentence contains an error, choose the one underlined part that must be changed to make the sentence correct. If the sentence is correct, select choice E.

23. If a submerged object's <u>density</u> is <u>less</u> than
              A   B
the surrounding fluid's density, the net

force is <u>upward</u> and the object <u>floats</u>.
         C   D
<u>No error</u>
  E

24. According to the <u>continuity equation</u>, as
                 A
water flows from a faucet, it <u>slows down</u>
                     B
due to <u>gravity</u> and the stream <u>narrows</u>.
       C   D
<u>No error</u>
  E

Name _______________________________ Class _________________ Date _______________

Holt Physics: Heat
Essay

DIRECTIONS: The essay gives you an opportunity to show how effectively you can develop and express ideas. You should, therefore, take care to develop your ideas, present concepts logically and clearly, and use language precisely.

Your essay must be written on your own paper. You may use both sides of a single sheet of notebook paper. You will have enough space if you write on every line, avoid wide margins, and keep your handwriting to a reasonable size. Remember that people who are not familiar with your handwriting will read what you write. Try to write or print so that what you are writing is legible to those readers.

IMPORTANT REMINDERS:
- **A pencil is required for the essay.** An essay written in ink will receive a score of zero.
- **Do not write your essay in your test book.** You will receive credit only for what you write on a single sheet of notebook paper.
- **An off-topic essay will receive a score of zero.**

Think carefully about the concept presented in the following passage and diagram and the assignment below.

The heating curve below shows the change in temperature of a sample of a substance as energy is added to the substance as heat. (Note that the horizontal scale of the graph is not uniform.)

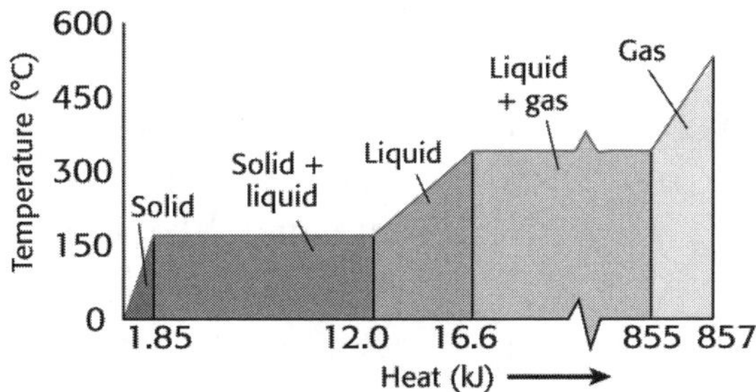

ASSIGNMENT: What happens to the substance as energy is added as heat? How does the temperature change as energy is added? What causes the horizontal parts of the graph? Plan and write an essay in which you address these questions. Support your explanation with reasoning and examples taken from your reading, studies, experience, or observations.

Holt Physics: Heat
Mathematics

DIRECTIONS: In this section, solve each problem using any available space on the page for scratch work. Then decide which of the choices given is best and fill in the corresponding circle on the answer sheet.

NOTES:
1. The use of a calculator is permitted. All numbers used are real numbers.
2. Figures that accompany problems in this test are intended to provide information useful in solving the problems. They are drawn as accurately as possible EXCEPT when it is stated in a specific problem that the figure is not drawn to scale. All figures lie in a plane unless otherwise indicated.

Reference Information

Celsius-Fahrenheit Conversion

$$T_F = \frac{9}{5}T_C + 32.0$$

Celsius-Kelvin Conversion

$$T = T_C + 273.15$$

Conservation of Energy

$$\Delta PE + \Delta KE + \Delta U = 0$$

Specific Heat Capacity

$$c_p = \frac{Q}{m\Delta T}$$

Substance	c_p (J/kg•°C)
aluminum	8.99×10^2
copper	3.87×10^2
ice	2.09×10^3
steam	2.01×10^3
water	4.186×10^3

1. One town's lowest temperature ever recorded is −29.5°F. What is this temperature on the Celsius scale?

   (A) −61.5°C

   (B) −34.2°C

   (C) −21.1°C

   (D) 239.0°C

   (E) 243.6°C

2. In one day, the temperatures of a desert range from 110°F in the afternoon to 55°F at night. What is this temperature range on the Kelvin scale?

   (A) 13 K to 43 K

   (B) 131 K to 230 K

   (C) 286 K to 316 K

   (D) 328 K to 383 K

   (E) 404 K to 503 K

GO ON TO THE NEXT PAGE

Mathematics *continued*

3. A room's temperature changes from 31.9°C to 22.4°C. What is the change in its temperature on the Kelvin scale?

   (A) −263.6 K

   (B) −17.2 K

   (C) −9.5 K

   (D) 263.6 K

   (E) 305.0 K

4. A man's body temperature goes from 98.6°F to a fever of 101.9°F. What is the change in his temperature on the Celsius scale?

   (A) 1.8°C

   (B) 3.3°C

   (C) 15.9°C

   (D) 275.0°C

   (E) 276.4°C

5. A carpenter swings a 2.5 kg mallet at a speed of 25 m/s to hit a peg into a hole. If one-fifth of the mallet's kinetic energy is converted to the internal energy of the mallet and peg, how much does the total internal energy increase?

   (A) 6.2 J

   (B) 160 J

   (C) 780 J

   (D) 1600 J

   (E) 3900 J

6. A 15 kg rock drops a distance of 21.0 m to the ground. If 45 percent of the initial potential energy goes into increasing the internal energy of the rock, what is the magnitude of that increase?

   (A) 1.4 J

   (B) 1.7 J

   (C) 3.1 J

   (D) 1400 J

   (E) 2100 J

7. What amount of internal energy is needed to raise the temperature of 0.50 kg of water from 79.5°F to 82.3°F?

   (A) 1600 J

   (B) 3100 J

   (C) 5400 J

   (D) 5900 J

   (E) 34 000 J

8. What mass of water at 25°C will cool a 2.0 kg copper block at 85°C to a final equilibrium temperature of 42°C?

   (A) 0.052 kg

   (B) 0.47 kg

   (C) 0.65 kg

   (D) 1.5 kg

   (E) 2.1 kg

GO ON TO THE NEXT PAGE

Mathematics *continued*

9. A 0.85 kg sample of an unknown liquid at 75.0°C is poured into 1.5 kg of water at 15.5°C. If the equilibrium temperature is 35.5°C, what is the specific heat capacity of the unknown liquid?

   (A) 3700 J/kg•°C

   (B) 22000 J/kg•°C

   (C) 1200 J/kg•°C

   (D) 7100 J/kg•°C

   (E) 7400 J/kg•°C

10. A solid aluminum machine part is placed in 350 g of water to cool. The water temperature changes by 4.76°C, and the temperature of the machine part changes by 57.5°C. What is the mass of the coin?

   (A) 7.41 g

   (B) 11.6 g

   (C) 19.6 g

   (D) 85.9 g

   (E) 135 g

Holt Physics: Heat
Sentence Completion

DIRECTIONS: For each question in this section, select the best answer from among the choices given and fill in the corresponding circle on the answer sheet.

11. The condition in which the temperature of two objects in physical contact with each other is the same is called ______.

    (A) calorimetry

    (B) phase change

    (C) thermal conduction

    (D) thermal equilibrium

    (E) thermal expansion

12. The energy per unit mass that is transferred during a phase change of a substance is called ______.

    (A) internal energy

    (B) latent heat

    (C) specific heat capacity

    (D) temperature

    (E) thermal equilibrium

13. ______ is a measure of the average kinetic energy of the particles in a substance.

    (A) Temperature

    (B) Internal energy

    (C) Heat

    (D) Thermal equilibrium

    (E) Latent heat

14. When you place a metal pan on a hot stove burner, the pan's metal handle becomes hot even though it is far from the burner because of ______.

    (A) convection

    (B) electromagnetic radiation

    (C) phase change

    (D) thermal conduction

    (E) thermal insulation

Holt Physics: Heat
Reading Passage

The passage and diagram below are followed by questions based on their content. Answer the questions on the basis of what is <u>stated</u> or <u>implied</u> in the passage. For each question in this section, select the best answer from the choices given and fill in the corresponding circle on the answer sheet.

Questions 15–19 are based on the following passage and diagram.

The heating system in Angela's new house is centered around a large gas furnace that is located in the basement.
Line The furnace burns natural gas, a process
5 that releases both fumes and great amounts of heat. The fumes are channeled out of Angela's home through a narrow duct that opens up to the outside air above the roof. Meanwhile, the heat released as
10 the fuel burns is harnessed to warm the house.

The figure below shows how this process works. Air in the furnace is warmed by the burning gas reaction. A

15 fan blows this hot air out of the furnace into a system of insulated ducts. The ducts release warm air into each room of the house via vents on the floor. The warm air circulates throughout the rooms,
20 which heats them and their contents.

The objects in the room cool the air as they absorb energy from it. Rather than take fresh air from outdoors, intake vents located in the floors of each room take
25 in this slightly cooled air and return it to the furnace. In this way, energy is conserved as the air is circulated throughout the heating system and house over and over again.

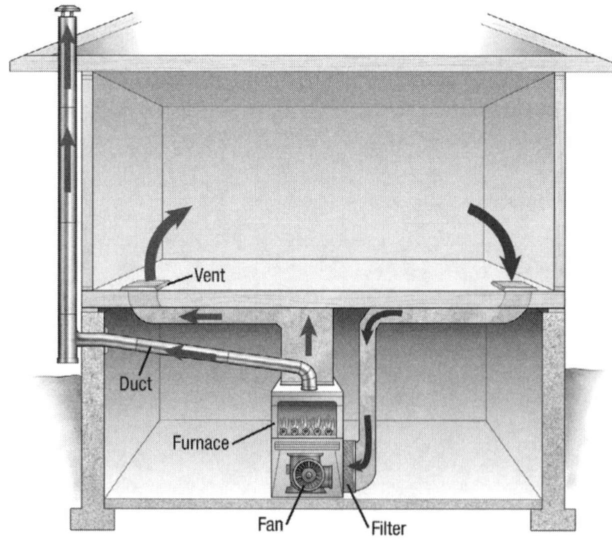

GO ON TO THE NEXT PAGE

15. What type of energy transfer is described in lines 18–20?

    (A) convection

    (B) electromagnetic radiation

    (C) phase change

    (D) thermal conduction

    (E) thermal insulation

16. What type of energy transfer heats a metal wrench that sits on top of the hot furnace?

    (A) convection

    (B) electromagnetic radiation

    (C) phase change

    (D) thermal conduction

    (E) thermal insulation

17. What happens to the warm air described in lines 16–22?

    (A) Its temperature remains constant until it reenters the furnace.

    (B) It is warmed by the room's contents to the equilibrium temperature.

    (C) It is warmed by the room's contents to their initial temperature.

    (D) It is cooled by the room's contents to the equilibrium temperature.

    (E) It is cooled by the room's contents to their initial temperature.

18. In line 27, the term "conserved" means

    (A) stored

    (B) released

    (C) not wasted

    (D) made new again

    (E) neither created nor destroyed

19. Heating ducts are often covered with materials that transfer heat energy slowly in order to prevent the air inside from losing heat before warming the house. What kinds of materials would work best for preventing heat loss?

    (A) furnaces

    (B) heat engines

    (C) radiators

    (D) thermal conductors

    (E) thermal insulators

Holt Physics: Heat
Improving Sentences

DIRECTIONS: For each question in this section, select the best answer from among the choices given and fill in the corresponding circle on the answer sheet.

Part of each sentence in items 20 and 21 is underlined. Below each sentence are five ways of phrasing the underlined material. Choice A repeats the original phrasing; the other four choices are different. Choose the answer you think produces the most accurate sentence.

20. The absolute temperature scale has <u>only values greater than 273.15</u>.

   (A) only values greater than 273.15

   (B) only positive values

   (C) only negative values

   (D) only whole number values

   (E) a value of 100 for boiling water

21. Heat is energy that is transferred from objects <u>at freezing temperatures to liquids</u>.

   (A) at freezing temperatures to liquids

   (B) that are in motion to objects that are at rest

   (C) that are at rest to objects that are in motion

   (D) at lower temperatures to objects at higher temperatures

   (E) at higher temperatures to objects at lower temperatures

Each sentence in items 22–24 contains either a single error or no error at all. If the sentence contains an error, choose the one underlined part that must be changed to make the sentence correct. If the sentence is correct, select choice E.

22. When a gas at constant <u>pressure</u> increases
                       A
   in <u>temperature</u>, the <u>volume</u> of the gas
         B   C
  <u>decreases</u>. <u>No error</u>
     D   E

23. A substance with a <u>high</u> specific heat
               A
  capacity will absorb <u>less</u> heat energy than
              B
  a substance with a <u>low</u> specific heat
            C
  capacity to undergo the same change in

  <u>temperature</u>. <u>No error</u>
     D   E

24. For a closed system, the sum of the

  changes in <u>kinetic energy</u>, <u>potential energy</u>,
           A   B
  and <u>internal energy</u> must equal <u>zero</u>.
      C   D
  <u>No error</u>
    E

Holt Physics: Thermodynamics
Essay

DIRECTIONS: The essay gives you an opportunity to show how effectively you can develop and express ideas. You should, therefore, take care to develop your ideas, present concepts logically and clearly, and use language precisely.

Your essay must be written on your own paper. You may use both sides of a single sheet of notebook paper. You will have enough space if you write on every line, avoid wide margins, and keep your handwriting to a reasonable size. Remember that people who are not familiar with your handwriting will read what you write. Try to write or print so that what you are writing is legible to those readers.

IMPORTANT REMINDERS:
- **A pencil is required for the essay.** An essay written in ink will receive a score of zero.
- **Do not write your essay in your test book.** You will receive credit only for what you write on a single sheet of notebook paper.
- **An off-topic essay will receive a score of zero.**

Think carefully about the concept presented in the following passage and the assignment below.

A heat engine uses heat to do work, but it cannot transfer all energy as heat to do work. According to the second law of thermodynamics, "No cyclic process that converts heat entirely into work is possible." A system's ability to do work and the direction of energy transfer are related to a system's entropy.

ASSIGNMENT: What is entropy? How can the second law of thermodynamics be expressed in terms of entropy change? How does this law explain the entropy of a system that includes water in an ice-cube tray in your kitchen's freezer? Plan and write an essay in which you address these questions. Support your explanation with reasoning and examples taken from your reading, studies, experience, or observations.

Mathematics

DIRECTIONS: In this section, solve each problem using any available space on the page for scratch work. Then decide which of the choices given is best and fill in the corresponding circle on the answer sheet.

NOTES:
1. The use of a calculator is permitted. All numbers used are real numbers.
2. Figures that accompany problems in this test are intended to provide information useful in solving the problems. They are drawn as accurately as possible EXCEPT when it is stated in a specific problem that the figure is not drawn to scale. All figures lie in a plane unless otherwise indicated.

Reference Information

Work Done by a Gas

$W = P\Delta V$

The First Law of Thermodynamics

$\Delta U = Q - W$

Efficiency of a Heat Engine

$eff = \dfrac{W_{net}}{Q_h} = \dfrac{Q_h - Q_c}{Q_h} = 1 - \dfrac{Q_c}{Q_h}$

Area of a Circle

$A = \pi r^2$

1. A 2.5 m^3 volume of gas has a pressure of 4.3×10^5 Pa. What is the work done by the gas if it expands at constant pressure to 3.5 times its initial volume?

   (A) 4.3×10^5 J

   (B) 1.1×10^6 J

   (C) 1.5×10^6 J

   (D) 2.7×10^6 J

   (E) 3.8×10^6 J

2. An enclosed sample of gas kept at a constant pressure of 1505 kPa changes volume from 6.225×10^{-4} m^3 to 1.500×10^{-4} m^3. How much work is done?

   (A) -1405 J

   (B) -1163 J

   (C) -936.9 J

   (D) -711.1 J

   (E) -0.7111 J

GO ON TO THE NEXT PAGE

Mathematics *continued*

3. A balloon is inflated with gas at a constant pressure of 240 kPa. If the balloon inflates from a volume of 2.5×10^{-4} m^3 to 6.0×10^{-4} m^3, how much work is done on the surrounding air by the gas-filled balloon during this expansion?

   (A) 84 J

   (B) 100 J

   (C) 200 J

   (D) 360 J

   (E) 580 J

4. A gas moves into a cylinder at a constant pressure and does 1.5 J of work on a piston. The diameter of the piston is 3.4 cm, and the piston travels 4.5 cm. What is the pressure of the gas?

   (A) 310 Pa

   (B) 980 Pa

   (C) 9200 Pa

   (D) 29 000 Pa

   (E) 37 000 Pa

5. Heat is added to a system, and the system does 35.0 J of work. If the internal energy increases by 17.0 J, how much heat was added to the system?

   (A) 2.06 J

   (B) 18.0 J

   (C) 52.0 J

   (D) 254 J

   (E) 595 J

6. The internal energy of a system decreases by 45.0 J. If 15.0 J of work is done by the system, how much energy is transferred to the system as heat?

   (A) −675 J

   (B) −180 J

   (C) −60.0 J

   (D) −30.0 J

   (E) −3.00 J

7. The internal energy of a gas decreases by 220 J. If the process is adiabatic, how much work is done by the gas?

   (A) 15 J

   (B) 110 J

   (C) 220 J

   (D) 440 J

   (E) 630 J

8. If a heat engine takes in 4565 kJ and gives up 2955 kJ during one cycle, what is the engine's efficiency?

   (A) 0.2955

   (B) 0.3527

   (C) 0.4552

   (D) 0.5448

   (E) 0.6473

GO ON TO THE NEXT PAGE

Mathematics *continued*

9. If a heat engine has an efficiency of 19 percent and loses 365 J during each cycle, how much work is done by the engine?

   (A) 86 J

   (B) 370 J

   (C) 450 J

   (D) 1500 J

   (E) 1900 J

10. A heat engine performs 1650 J of work in each cycle with an efficiency of 28.0 percent. How much energy is transferred from the engine to the exhaust and cooling system as heat?

   (A) 462 J

   (B) 1190 J

   (C) 1650 J

   (D) 4240 J

   (E) 5890 J

Holt Physics: Thermodynamics
Sentence Completion

DIRECTIONS: For each question in this section, select the best answer from among the choices given and fill in the corresponding circle on the answer sheet.

11. Work done on or by a gas is dependent on _______ and _______ change.

    (A) heat . . volume

    (B) volume . . heat

    (C) pressure . . volume

    (D) volume . . pressure

    (E) internal energy . . pressure

12. A thermodynamic process that takes place at constant volume so that no work is done on or by the system is called a(n) _______.

    (A) adiabatic process

    (B) cyclic process

    (C) dynamic process

    (D) isothermal process

    (E) isovolumetric process

13. A thermodynamic process during which no energy is transferred to or from the system as heat is called a(n) _______.

    (A) adiabatic process

    (B) cyclic process

    (C) dynamic process

    (D) isothermal process

    (E) isovolumetric process

14. The entropy of a system can increase or decrease, but the total entropy of the universe is always _______.

    (A) decreasing

    (B) increasing

    (C) negative

    (D) one

    (E) zero

15. A(n) _______ returns a system to conditions identical to those it had before the process began, so its internal energy is unchanged.

    (A) adiabatic process

    (B) cyclic process

    (C) dynamic process

    (D) isothermal process

    (E) isovolumetric process

Holt Physics: Thermodynamics
Reading Passage

The passage below is followed by questions based on its content. Answer the questions on the basis of what is <u>stated</u> or <u>implied</u> in the passages For each question in this section, select the best answer from the choices given and fill in the corresponding circle on the answer sheet.

Questions 16–20 are based on the following passage.

With the fossil fuels used to run electrical generators rapidly diminishing, finding new methods of producing electricity has become an important priority. While water and wind power are already in use, one promising source of electricity may be something Earth has more than enough of—sunlight.

Engineers are working to harness the sun's energy to generate electricity efficiently through technology such as the Stirling engine, a machine that was invented by Robert Stirling in 1816. A large dish-shaped mirror is used to reflect sunlight onto an absorber, which collects the energy and uses it to increase the internal energy of helium inside the engine. At that point, the engine works much like an automobile engine, with the heated helium gas being used to move a piston. But instead of spinning a set of wheels, this piston turns an electric generator.

The Stirling engine operates very efficiently. It is ideal for remote locations, where normal power lines cannot be run, or to power-specific devices, such as water pumps for agricultural purposes.

Another type of solar power plant in development uses the sun's energy to melt large quantities of salt. The energy transferred by heat from the salt is then used to generate steam, which can turn a turbine to make electricity. Also, the hot salt can be kept in insulated tanks, enabling its high internal energy to be stored. Previous solar power systems simply heated water to the boiling point, but the water boiled only while the sun was shining. A new, salt-heated device stores energy more efficiently than water and maintains the higher temperature long enough to produce electricity even at night.

Greg Kolb, an engineer at Sandia National Laboratories, in Albuquerque, New Mexico, envisions such a power source replacing the central power stations we have today. "Imagine a tower about the size of the Washington Monument surrounded by a field of mirrors on the ground approximately one square mile in area," Kolb says. "The mirrors are reflecting the sunlight to the top of the tower, where all the light is focused and the energy is absorbed in a large heat exchanger." The engineer estimates that about 10 000 such setups spread throughout the nation could provide as much energy as the United States consumes annually.

GO ON TO THE NEXT PAGE

Reading Passage *continued*

16. What source of energy does the engine described in lines 9–23 use?

    (A) sunlight

    (B) melting salt

    (C) burning helium

    (D) burning fossil fuels

    (E) wind and water power

17. According to lines 1–8, a decrease in what natural resource is causing engineers to look for new ways to generate electricity?

    (A) fossil fuels

    (B) helium

    (C) salt

    (D) sunlight

    (E) water

18. According to lines 9–23, how is the Stirling engine similar to an automobile engine?

    (A) Helium is burned as fuel.

    (B) Gasoline is burned as fuel.

    (C) Sunlight is used to heat a gas.

    (D) A heated gas moves a piston.

    (E) A piston spins a set of wheels.

19. What turns the turbine that generates electricity in the solar power plant described in lines 29–44?

    (A) wind

    (B) steam

    (C) helium

    (D) saltwater

    (E) melted salt

20. What does the phrase "more efficiently" in line 41 most likely refer to?

    (A) producing more work

    (B) in a shorter period of time

    (C) using fewer natural resources

    (D) losing less heat to the environment

    (E) having a greater mechanical advantage

Holt Physics: Thermodynamics
Improving Sentences

DIRECTIONS: For each question in this section, select the best answer from among the choices given and fill in the corresponding circle on the answer sheet.

Part of each sentence in items 21 and 22 is underlined. Below each sentence are five ways of phrasing the underlined material. Choice A repeats the original phrasing; the other four choices are different. Choose the answer you think produces the most accurate sentence.

21. When volume does not change in a process, <u>no heat is lost</u>.

    (A) no heat is lost

    (B) no heat is gained

    (C) no work is done

    (D) work is maximized

    (E) efficiency is maximized

22. The larger the difference between the energy transferred as heat into an engine and out of the engine, <u>the greater the amount of heat lost to the environment</u>.

    (A) the greater the amount of heat lost to the environment

    (B) the smaller the internal energy of the engine

    (C) the smaller the efficiency of the engine

    (D) the less work the engine can do in each cycle

    (E) the more work the engine can do in each cycle

Each sentence in items 23 and 24 contains either a single error or no error at all. If the sentence contains an error, choose the one underlined part that must be changed to make the sentence correct. If the sentence is correct, select choice E.

23. According to the <u>second</u> law of
                        A
    thermodynamics, a system's <u>internal</u>
                               B
    energy can be changed by transferring
    energy as either <u>work,</u> <u>heat,</u> or a
                     C   D
    combination of the two. <u>No error</u>
                             E

24. The <u>greater</u> the <u>entropy</u> of a <u>system</u> is, the
          A   B   C
    greater the system's <u>order</u>. <u>No error</u>
                        D   E

Holt Physics: Vibrations and Waves
Essay

DIRECTIONS: The essay gives you an opportunity to show how effectively you can develop and express ideas. You should, therefore, take care to develop your ideas, present concepts logically and clearly, and use language precisely.

Your essay must be written on your own paper. You may use both sides of a single sheet of notebook paper. You will have enough space if you write on every line, avoid wide margins, and keep your handwriting to a reasonable size. Remember that people who are not familiar with your handwriting will read what you write. Try to write or print so that what you are writing is legible to those readers.

IMPORTANT REMINDERS:

- **A pencil is required for the essay.** An essay written in ink will receive a score of zero.
- **Do not write your essay in your test book.** You will receive credit only for what you write on a single sheet of notebook paper.
- **An off-topic essay will receive a score of zero.**

Think carefully about the concept presented in the following passage and the assignment below.

On the morning of November 7, 1940, the Tacoma Narrows Bridge, a 1600-meter suspension bridge connecting the cities of Tacoma and Gig Harbor in the state of Washington, began to rock violently due to vibrations caused by wind gusts. The vibrations created a standing wave in the bridge, such that certain portions of the bridge experienced constructive interference and vibrated far from their rest positions, while other portions of the bridge experienced destructive interference and remained in their rest positions. Eventually, the standing wave caused the bridge to collapse.

ASSIGNMENT: What is a standing wave? What characteristics of a standing wave are described in the passage? Why might a standing wave cause a bridge to collapse? Plan and write an essay in which you address these questions. Support your explanation with reasoning and examples taken from your reading, studies, experience, or observations.

Holt Physics: Vibrations and Waves
Mathematics

DIRECTIONS: In this section, solve each problem using any available space on the page for scratch work. Then decide which of the choices given is best and fill in the corresponding circle on the answer sheet.

NOTES:
1. The use of a calculator is permitted. All numbers used are real numbers.
2. Figures that accompany problems in this test are intended to provide information useful in solving the problems. They are drawn as accurately as possible EXCEPT when it is stated in a specific problem that the figure is not drawn to scale. All figures lie in a plane unless otherwise indicated.

Reference Information

$a_g = 9.81$ m/s^2

Hooke's Law
$F_{elastic} = -kx$

Wave Equation
$v = f\lambda$

Simple Pendulum in Simple Harmonic Motion
$$T = 2\pi\sqrt{\frac{L}{a_g}}$$

Mass-Spring System in Simple Harmonic Motion
$$T = 2\pi\sqrt{\frac{m}{k}}$$

1. If a mass of 0.75 kg attached to a vertical spring stretches the spring 5.0 m from its original equilibrium position, what is the spring constant?

   (A) 0.15 N/m

   (B) 1.5 N/m

   (C) 2.0 N/m

   (D) 2.4 N/m

   (E) 150 N/m

2. What is the length of a pendulum that oscillates with a frequency of 0.21 Hz?

   (A) 0.011 m

   (B) 0.33 m

   (C) 2.1 m

   (D) 4.8 m

   (E) 5.6 m

3. What is the period of a mass-spring system with a mass of 25.0 kg and a spring constant of 1.25 N/m?

   (A) 0.990 s

   (B) 1.40 s

   (C) 19.8 s

   (D) 28.1 s

   (E) 631 s

4. What is the period of a metronome that vibrates at a frequency of 4.0 Hz?

   (A) 0.25 s

   (B) 0.40 s

   (C) 2.0 s

   (D) 15 s

   (E) 240 s

GO ON TO THE NEXT PAGE

Mathematics *continued*

Questions 5–8 are based on the following illustration of a wave traveling in the positive *x* direction with a frequency of 33.3 Hz.

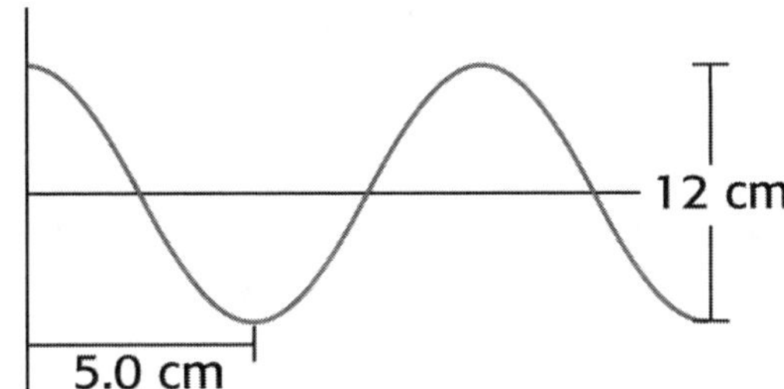

5. What is the amplitude of the wave?

   (A) 5.0 cm

   (B) 6.0 cm

   (C) 10.0 cm

   (D) 12.0 cm

   (E) 20.0 cm

6. What is the wavelength of the wave?

   (A) 5.0 cm

   (B) 6.0 cm

   (C) 10.0 cm

   (D) 12.0 cm

   (E) 20.0 cm

7. What is the period of the wave?

   (A) 0.0300 s

   (B) 3.00 s

   (C) 33.3 s

   (D) 166 s

   (E) 333 s

8. What is the speed of the wave?

   (A) 0.0300 m/s

   (B) 3.00 m/s

   (C) 33.3 m/s

   (D) 166 m/s

   (E) 333 m/s

9. A sound wave has a frequency of 3400 Hz and a wavelength of 1.5 m in a certain medium. What is the speed of the wave in that medium?

   (A) 4.4×10^{-4} m/s

   (B) 2.9×10^{-4} m/s

   (C) 1.9 m/s

   (D) 2300 m/s

   (E) 5100 m/s

10. A wave of frequency 42.5 Hz travels at a speed of 3.5 m/s. What is the wavelength of the wave?

   (A) 0.082 cm

   (B) 8.2 cm

   (C) 12 cm

   (D) 150 cm

   (E) 15,000 cm

GO ON TO THE NEXT PAGE

Holt Physics: Vibrations and Waves
Sentence Completion

DIRECTIONS: For each question in this section, select the best answer from among the choices given and fill in the corresponding circle on the answer sheet.

11. A pendulum's _______ stays the same even as its kinetic energy increases (if friction is disregarded).

    (A) speed

    (B) height

    (C) displacement

    (D) potential energy

    (E) total mechanical energy

12. According to Hooke's law, spring force can be calculated by knowing the spring constant and the _______ of the spring.

    (A) mass

    (B) thickness

    (C) displacement

    (D) mechanical energy

    (E) equilibrium length

13. The period of a simple pendulum in simple harmonic motion is equal to 2π multiplied by the square root of the _______ of the pendulum divided by the square root of its _______.

    (A) length . . mass

    (B) mass . . frequency

    (C) frequency . . length

    (D) free-fall acceleration . . mass

    (E) length . . free-fall acceleration

14. Vibrations in a _______ wave are always parallel to the direction of wave motion, while vibrations in a _______ are perpendicular to the direction of wave motion.

    (A) longitudinal . . transverse

    (B) transverse . . longitudinal

    (C) mechanical . . longitudinal

    (D) transverse . . electromagnetic

    (E) mechanical . . electromagnetic

15. When the compression of one longitudinal wave and the rarefaction of another combine, there is _______.

    (A) reflection

    (B) an antinode

    (C) a standing wave

    (D) destructive interference

    (E) constructive interference

Holt Physics: Vibrations and Waves
Reading Passages

The passages below are followed by questions based on their content; questions following a pair of related passages may also be based on the relationship between the paired passages. Answer the questions on the basis of what is <u>stated</u> or <u>implied</u> in the passages. For each question in this section, select the best answer from the choices given and fill in the corresponding circle on the answer sheet.

Questions 16-17 are based on the following passage.

Tsunamis are large, often devastating ocean waves that are triggered by great disturbances to land or water. They
Line may be caused by earthquakes, landslides,
5 volcanoes, meteorite strikes, or significant explosions that take place on land or underwater. The wave that forms near the original location of the disturbance has a relatively small amplitude and large
10 wavelength. However, as the tsunami nears land, its amplitude grows and its wavelength shortens, causing destructive waves that can be dozens of meters high.

16. Lines 1-3 suggest that the term "tsunami" might also be defined as

(A) any wave that moves through land

(B) an earthquake occurring underwater

(C) any wave that moves through water

(D) an ocean wave that takes place underwater

(E) the motion of a great disturbance through water

17. According to lines 11-13, what amplitude can a tsunami reach at shore?

(A) 0.3 meters

(B) 3 meters

(C) 36 meters

(D) 360 meters

(E) 3600 meters

Questions 18-20 are based on the following passage.

When waves meet one another, they can interact in different ways. The overlapping of two or more waves is
Line called superposition. Superposition can
5 involve constructive or destructive interference. When the superposition of waves results in a resultant wave with an amplitude that is larger than either of the combining waves, the phenomenon is
10 called constructive interference. When the superposition of waves results in a resultant wave with an amplitude that is smaller than either of the original waves, the phenomenon is called destructive
15 interference.

One laboratory demonstration of a wave interaction involves two partners holding each end of the rope. Both people generate transverse waves of equal
20 amplitude that move toward each other in the rope. At the moment when a crest and a trough of the waves first overlap in the middle of the rope, the amplitude becomes zero.

18. The description of the rope experiment described in lines 16-21 suggests that

(A) the waves reflected

(B) the waves formed nodes

(C) the waves interfered destructively

(D) the waves interfered constructively

(E) the waves formed a standing wave

GO ON TO THE NEXT PAGE

19. In line 14, the word "destructive" means

    (A) critical

    (B) vicious

    (C) unhelpful

    (D) causing ruin

    (E) making smaller

20. The passage implies that which two words are synonyms?

    (A) resultant and original

    (B) wave and interference

    (C) phenomenon and amplitude

    (D) constructive and destructive

    (E) overlapping and superposition

GO ON TO THE NEXT PAGE

Holt Physics: Vibrations and Waves
Improving Sentences

DIRECTIONS: For each question in this section, select the best answer from among the choices given and fill in the corresponding circle on the answer sheet.

Part of each sentence in items 21 and 22 is underlined. Below each sentence are five ways of phrasing the underlined material. Choice A repeats the original phrasing; the other four choices are different. Choose the answer you think produces the most accurate sentence.

21. Wave speed equals <u>amplitude</u> multiplied by wavelength.

    (A) amplitude

    (B) energy

    (C) frequency

    (D) medium

    (E) period

22. In a standing wave on a guitar string, the antinodes are the points where the string vibrates with the largest <u>wavelength</u>.

    (A) wavelength

    (B) amplitude

    (C) frequency

    (D) period

    (E) speed

Each sentence in items 23 and 24 contains either a single error or no error at all. If the sentence contains an error, choose the one underlined part that must be changed to make the sentence correct. If the sentence is correct, select choice E.

23. <u>Mechanical</u> waves transfer <u>matter</u> by
        A   B
    vibrating <u>particles</u> that return to their
            C
    original <u>equilibrium</u> positions rather than
           D
    by carrying the particles along with the

    wave. <u>No error</u>
        E

24. <u>Mechanical</u> waves require a <u>medium</u>,
        A   B
    while <u>electromagnetic</u> waves can travel
          C
    through a <u>vacuum</u>. <u>No error</u>
        D   E

Holt Physics: Sound
Essay

DIRECTIONS: The essay gives you an opportunity to show how effectively you can develop and express ideas. You should, therefore, take care to develop your ideas, present concepts logically and clearly, and use language precisely.

Your essay must be written on your own paper. You may use both sides of a single sheet of notebook paper. You will have enough space if you write on every line, avoid wide margins, and keep your handwriting to a reasonable size. Remember that people who are not familiar with your handwriting will read what you write. Try to write or print so that what you are writing is legible to those readers.

IMPORTANT REMINDERS:

- **A pencil is required for the essay.** An essay written in ink will receive a score of zero.
- **Do not write your essay in your test book.** You will receive credit only for what you write on a single sheet of notebook paper.
- **An off-topic essay will receive a score of zero.**

> **Think carefully about the concept presented in the following passage and diagram and the assignment below.**
>
> The diagram below shows two stationary observers (represented by points *A* and *B*) and a moving sound source (represented by a sphere). The sound source is moving towards observer *B*.
>
> 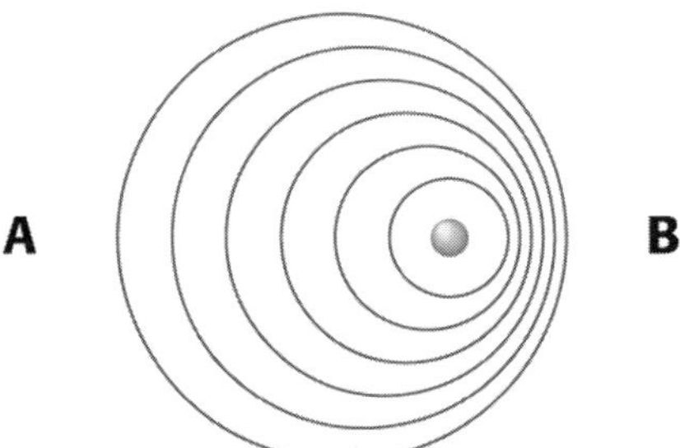
>
>
> **ASSIGNMENT: Which observer observes the greater frequency? How does this affect the relative pitches that each observer hears? How does the actual frequency of the sound source compare to that observed by each observer? What is the Doppler effect and how does it play a role in this situation? Plan and write an essay in which you address these questions. Support your explanation with reasoning and examples taken from your reading, studies, experience, or observations.**

Holt Physics: Sound
Mathematics

DIRECTIONS: In this section, solve each problem using any available space on the page for scratch work. Then decide which of the choices given is best and fill in the corresponding circle on the answer sheet.

NOTES:
1. The use of a calculator is permitted. All numbers used are real numbers.
2. Figures that accompany problems in this test are intended to provide information useful in solving the problems. They are drawn as accurately as possible EXCEPT when it is stated in a specific problem that the figure is not drawn to scale. All figures lie in a plane unless otherwise indicated.

Reference Information

Wave Equation

$$v = f\lambda$$

Harmonic Series of Standing Waves on a Vibrating String

$$f_n = n\frac{v}{2L} \quad n = 1, 2, 3, \ldots$$

Harmonic Series of a Pipe Closed at One End

$$f_n = n\frac{v}{4L} \quad n = 1, 3, 5, \ldots$$

Intensity of a Spherical Wave

$$\text{intensity} = \frac{P}{4\pi r^2}$$

Harmonic Series of a Pipe Open at Both Ends

$$f_n = n\frac{v}{2L} \quad n = 1, 2, 3, \ldots$$

1. What is the intensity of the sound waves at a distance of 15.0 m from a speaker when the speaker's power output is 25 W?

   (A) 8.8×10^{-3} W/m^2
   (B) 3.5×10^{-2} W/m^2
   (C) 1.1×10^{-1} W/m^2
   (D) 6.0×10^{-1} W/m^2
   (E) 1.7×10^{0} W/m^2

2. At a rock concert, the power output of the speakers is 195.0 W. What is the intensity of the emitted sound waves to a person in the audience who is standing 35.5 m from the speakers?

   (A) 1.23×10^{-2} W/m^2
   (B) 4.93×10^{-2} W/m^2
   (C) 1.55×10^{-1} W/m^2
   (D) 4.37×10^{-1} W/m^2
   (E) 5.49×10^{0} W/m^2

GO ON TO THE NEXT PAGE

Mathematics *continued*

3. An animal makes a sound that has an intensity of 9.4×10^{-8} W/m^2 at a distance of 5.0 m. How much sound power does the animal generate?

   (A) 3.0×10^{-10} W

   (B) 2.4×10^{-6} W

   (C) 5.9×10^{-6} W

   (D) 4.7×10^{-7} W

   (E) 3.0×10^{-5} W

4. How much power is radiated as sound from a siren that has an intensity of 6.3×10^{-5} W/m^2 at a distance of 55 m?

   (A) 0.19 W

   (B) 1.9 W

   (C) 2.4 W

   (D) 3.5 W

   (E) 8.7 W

5. The power output of a doorbell is 0.25 W. At what distance is the sound intensity of the doorbell 3.3×10^{-4} W/m^2?

   (A) 7.8 m

   (B) 28 m

   (C) 49 m

   (D) 61 m

   (E) 760 m

6. Sound travels at a speed of 354 m/s in a 0.750 m long pipe that is closed at one end. What is the frequency of the third harmonic in the pipe?

   (A) 118 Hz

   (B) 236 Hz

   (C) 354 Hz

   (D) 472 Hz

   (E) 708 Hz

7. What is the frequency of the fifth harmonic of a 25.0 cm long pitch pipe that is open at both ends, when the speed of sound in the pipe is 336 m/s?

   (A) 16.8 Hz

   (B) 33.6 Hz

   (C) 336 Hz

   (D) 1680 Hz

   (E) 3360 Hz

8. When the wind blows, a standing wave is created in a pipe that is open at both ends. The length of the pipe is 2.4 m and the speed of sound in the pipe is 352 m/s. What is the fundamental frequency of the pipe?

   (A) 6.8 Hz

   (B) 37 Hz

   (C) 73 Hz

   (D) 150 Hz

   (E) 350 Hz

GO ON TO THE NEXT PAGE

Mathematics *continued*

9. What is the fundamental frequency of a guitar string when the speed of waves on the string is 640 m/s and the effective string length is 85.0 cm?

   (A) 190 Hz

   (B) 380 Hz

   (C) 560 Hz

   (D) 640 Hz

   (E) 750 Hz

10. A ukulele string that is 38.0 cm long has a fundamental frequency of 850 Hz. What is the speed of the waves on this string?

    (A) 22 m/s

    (B) 45 m/s

    (C) 320 m/s

    (D) 650 m/s

    (E) 1300 m/s

Questions 11 and 12 are based on the following figure that shows a stretched string vibrating in one of its modes.

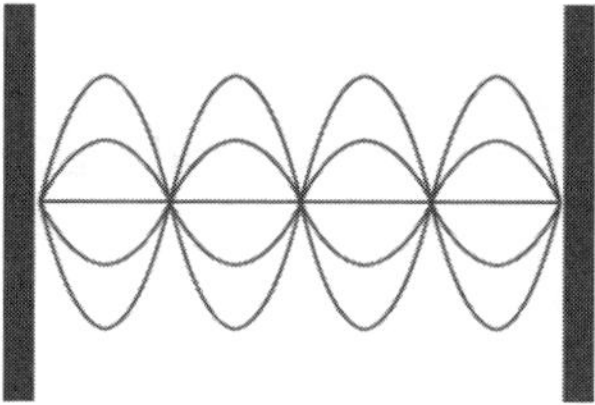

11. If the length of the string is 0.96 m, what is the wavelength of the wave on the string?

    (A) 0.24 m

    (B) 0.48 m

    (C) 0.96 m

    (D) 3.8 m

    (E) 4.0 m

12. What harmonic is represented?

    (A) fundamental frequency

    (B) second harmonic

    (C) third harmonic

    (D) fourth harmonic

    (E) fifth harmonic

Holt Physics: Sound
Sentence Completion

DIRECTIONS: For each question in this section, select the best answer from among the choices given and fill in the corresponding circle on the answer sheet.

13. The frequency of a sound wave determines its ______.

   (A) amplitude

   (B) intensity

   (C) power

   (D) pitch

   (E) speed

14. The periodic variation in the amplitude of a wave that is the superposition of two waves of slightly different frequencies is called a ______.

   (A) antinode

   (B) beat

   (C) node

   (D) pitch

   (E) standing wave

15. The sound quality of an instrument is also called its ______.

   (A) harmonics

   (B) pitch

   (C) rarefaction

   (D) resonance

   (E) timbre

16. Air vibrating in a pipe open at both ends produces ______ harmonics, while air vibrating in a pipe closed at one end produces ______ harmonics.

   (A) all . . only odd

   (B) all . . only even

   (C) only even . . all

   (D) only even. . only odd

   (E) only odd. . only even

Holt Physics: Sound
Reading Passages

The passages below are followed by questions based on their content; questions following a pair of related passages may also be based on the relationship between the paired passages. Answer the questions on the basis of what is <u>stated</u> or <u>implied</u> in the passages. For each question in this section, select the best answer from the choices given and fill in the corresponding circle on the answer sheet.

Questions 17–20 are based on the following passages.

Passage 1

    Bats, whales, dolphins, and some birds use a sound-navigation technique called echolocation to find their way through their environment and to hunt for food. In echolocation, the animal sends out sound waves, which reflect off nearby surfaces or objects, such as prey. The animal detects the reflected sound waves, or echoes, and processes the time delay of the echoes to determine how far away the object or surface is. Echoes that take longer to return are generally farther away.

    Echolocating animals receive sounds in both ears. Because the two ears are set apart on the animal's head, an echo signal coming from one direction will be received by each ear at different times. The animal's brain can process this information to determine from which direction the echo came, much in the same way that human binocular vision can determine distance based on the difference in the light information received by each eye. If a signal takes longer to arrive at one ear than the other, then the signal reflected off of an object that is located farther away from that ear than the other.

Passage 2

    Submarines and other boats can use sound waves to navigate underwater through a technique called sonar. Sonar stands for **SO**und **N**avigation **A**nd **R**anging. In the same way that bats send and receive sound signals to determine an object's location, a sonar device can locate underwater surfaces using sonic signals called "pings."

    A sonar device has two parts, a transmitter and a receiver. The transmitter sends out sound waves, which can reflect off objects or the ocean floor. The sound waves that reflect back towards the boat are detected by the receiver. Sound traveling through a fairly consistent medium, such as ocean water, has a nearly constant speed. Thus, the length of time it takes the sound wave to travel from the transmitter to a reflective surface and back to the receiver is directly related to the total distance the sound wave traveled. A sonar device can interpret the reflected pings and make a map that shows the distances of reflected surfaces.

    In this way, a submarine's navigator can use sonar to detect crevices, protrusions, and sunken objects on the ocean floor. The navigator can also detect the presence of nearby boats and large marine animals.

GO ON TO THE NEXT PAGE

17. According to lines 14–29 of Passage 1, the brains of echolocating animals compare the signals received by both ears. What does the difference in these signals tell the animal?

    (A) how far away an object is

    (B) how large a prey animals is

    (C) from what direction an echo came

    (D) how high the pitch of the sound is

    (E) how fast the speed of sound travels

18. According to lines 14–24 of Passage 2, the time it takes for a ping's echo to reflect back to the receiver is related to the

    (A) size of the boat's transmitter

    (B) texture of a reflective surface

    (C) distance of a reflective surface

    (D) density of the reflective surface

    (E) density of the air inside the boat

19. According to the passages, what does the term "navigation" mean?

    (A) reading a map

    (B) hunting for food

    (C) flying through the air

    (D) swimming in the water

    (E) finding the way through an environment

20. Passage 1 describes echolocation, while Passage 2 describes sonar. How are these two techniques similar?

    (A) Both have names that are acronyms.

    (B) Both involve a transmitter and two receivers.

    (C) Both are used only by things that move around underwater.

    (D) Both involve the use of reflected sound waves to locate objects.

    (E) Both are technologies that humans have developed in the last century.

Holt Physics: Sound
Improving Sentences

DIRECTIONS: For each question in this section, select the best answer from among the choices given and fill in the corresponding circle on the answer sheet.

Part of each sentence in items 21 and 22 is underlined. Below each sentence are five ways of phrasing the underlined material. Choice A repeats the original phrasing; the other four choices are different. Choose the answer you think produces the most accurate sentence.

21. Sounds above an intensity of about 1.0 W/m^2 are <u>inaudible to most animals</u>.

    (A) inaudible to most animals

    (B) at the threshold of hearing

    (C) similar to the human voice

    (D) damaging to the human ear

    (E) below the threshold of hearing

22. When two vibrating tuning forks produce beats, the number of beats per second corresponds to the <u>difference between the intensities of the tuning forks</u>.

    (A) difference between the intensities of the tuning forks

    (B) sum of the lengths of the tuning forks

    (C) sum of the frequencies of the tuning forks

    (D) difference between the lengths of the tuning forks

    (E) difference between the frequencies of the tuning forks

Each sentence in items 23 and 24 contains either a single error or no error at all. If the sentence contains an error, choose the one underlined part that must be changed to make the sentence correct. If the sentence is correct, select choice E.

23. The <u>relative motion</u> between the <u>source</u> of
         A   B
    waves and <u>an observer</u> creates an apparent
             C
    <u>intensity</u> shift known as the Doppler
       D
    effect. <u>No error</u>
          E

24. <u>Decibel</u> level is a measure of <u>relative</u>
      A   B
    <u>intensity</u> on an <u>exponential</u> scale.
      C   D
    <u>No error</u>
     E

Holt Physics: Light and Reflection
Essay

DIRECTIONS: The essay gives you an opportunity to show how effectively you can develop and express ideas. You should, therefore, take care to develop your ideas, present concepts logically and clearly, and use language precisely.

Your essay must be written on your own paper. You may use both sides of a single sheet of notebook paper. You will have enough space if you write on every line, avoid wide margins, and keep your handwriting to a reasonable size. Remember that people who are not familiar with your handwriting will read what you write. Try to write or print so that what you are writing is legible to those readers.

IMPORTANT REMINDERS:

- **A pencil is required for the essay.** An essay written in ink will receive a score of zero.
- **Do not write your essay in your test book.** You will receive credit only for what you write on a single sheet of notebook paper.
- **An off-topic essay will receive a score of zero.**

Think carefully about the concept presented in the following passage and diagram and the assignment below.

The diagram below shows rays of light reflecting off of a surface.

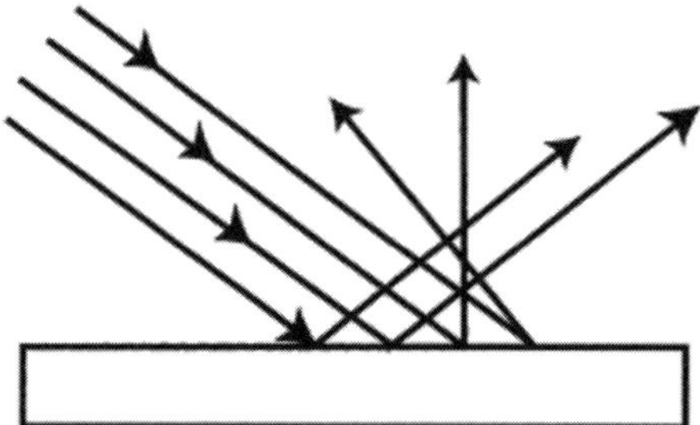

ASSIGNMENT: What happens to the incoming light rays after they hit the surface? What do the different angles of the reflected light rays tell you about the surface? What is the relationship between the angle of an incoming light ray and the angle of a reflected light ray for a smooth surface? Plan and write an essay in which you address these questions. Support your explanation with reasoning and examples taken from your reading, studies, experience, or observations.

Holt Physics: Light and Reflection
Mathematics

DIRECTIONS: In this section, solve each problem using any available space on the page for scratch work. Then decide which of the choices given is best and fill in the corresponding circle on the answer sheet.

NOTES:
1. The use of a calculator is permitted. All numbers used are real numbers.
2. Figures that accompany problems in this test are intended to provide information useful in solving the problems. They are drawn as accurately as possible EXCEPT when it is stated in a specific problem that the figure is not drawn to scale. All figures lie in a plane unless otherwise indicated.

Reference Information

Wave Speed Equation

$$c = f\lambda$$

Mirror Equation

$$\frac{1}{p} + \frac{1}{q} = \frac{1}{f} = \frac{2}{R}$$

Equation for Magnification

$$M = \frac{h'}{h} = -\frac{q}{p}$$

Speed of Light Traveling in a Vacuum

$$c = 3.00 \times 10^8 \text{ m/s}$$

1. Many television signals are transmitted through electromagnetic waves with frequencies from 3.0×10^7 Hz to 3.0×10^9 Hz. What is the longest wavelength associated with this frequency range?

   (A) 1.0×10^{-1} m

   (B) 1.0×10^1 m

   (C) 2.9×10^9 m

   (D) 3.0×10^9 m

   (E) 9.0×10^{17} m

2. Many cell phones communicate through microwaves that have frequencies near 8.00×10^8 Hz. What is the wavelength of these microwaves?

   (A) 2.40×10^{-8} m

   (B) 3.75×10^{-1} m

   (C) 5.00×10^8 m

   (D) 1.10×10^9 m

   (E) 2.40×10^{17} m

GO ON TO THE NEXT PAGE

3. What is the frequency of a radio wave that has a wavelength of 0.55 km?

  (A) 1.8×10^{-6} Hz

  (B) 5.5×10^{5} Hz

  (C) 5.4×10^{8} Hz

  (D) 7.5×10^{8} Hz

  (E) 1.6×10^{11} Hz

4. What is the frequency of a gamma ray that has a wavelength of 6.75×10^{-5} nm?

  (A) 2.02×10^{-5} Hz

  (B) 9.75×10^{3} Hz

  (C) 2.02×10^{4} Hz

  (D) 4.44×10^{12} Hz

  (E) 4.44×10^{21} Hz

5. A concave dental mirror has a focal length of 25 cm. What is the image position of a tooth placed 2.5 cm in front of the mirror?

  (A) 2.8 cm behind mirror

  (B) 2.8 cm in front of mirror

  (C) 22 cm behind mirror

  (D) 22 cm in front of mirror

  (E) 36 cm behind mirror

6. A concave mirror is designed so that an object 1.0 m in front of it produces a real image at a distance of 1.6 m in front of the mirror. What is the radius of curvature of the mirror?

  (A) 0.62 m

  (B) 1.2 m

  (C) 1.3 m

  (D) 2.7 m

  (E) 5.3 m

Questions 7 and 8 are based on the following figure that shows a ray of light reflecting off a plane mirror.

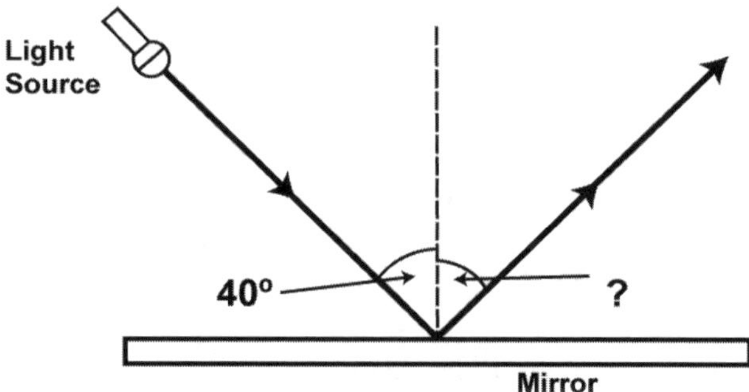

7. What is the measure of the angle of incidence in the diagram above?

  (A) 40°

  (B) 50°

  (C) 80°

  (D) 90°

  (E) 130°

8. What is the measure of the angle of reflection in the diagram above?

  (A) 40°

  (B) 50°

  (C) 80°

  (D) 90°

  (E) 130°

GO ON TO THE NEXT PAGE

Mathematics *continued*

Questions 9 and 10 are based on the following ray diagram showing a candle that is placed 50.0 cm from the reflecting surface of a concave spherical mirror. The radius of curvature of the mirror is 25.0 cm.

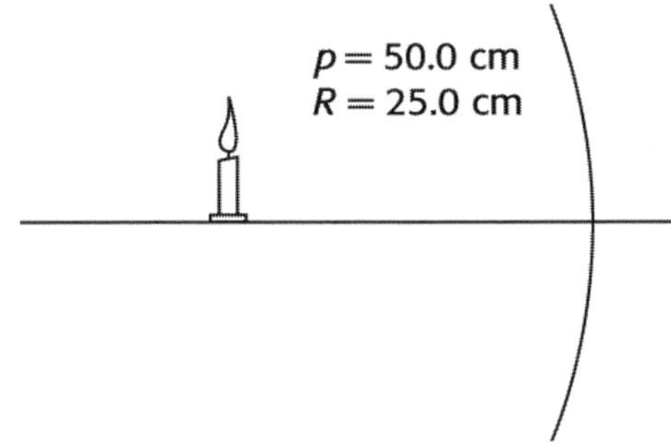

9. What is the focal length of the mirror?

   (A) 12.5 cm

   (B) 16.7 cm

   (C) 25.0 cm

   (D) 33.4 cm

   (E) 50.0 cm

10. If the candle is 20.0 cm tall, what is the image height?

   (A) −40.0 cm

   (B) −11.1 cm

   (C) −10.0 cm

   (D) −6.67 cm

   (E) −2.40 cm

11. A convex mirror of focal length 29 cm forms an image of a coffee mug at a distance of 15 cm behind the mirror. What is the magnification of the image?

   (A) 0.32

   (B) 0.48

   (C) 1.5

   (D) 2.1

   (E) 31

12. The image of a jar appears to be 23.5 cm tall in a convex security mirror. If the mirror's magnification is 0.75, what is the actual height of the jar?

   (A) 1.4 cm

   (B) 18 cm

   (C) 24 cm

   (D) 31 cm

   (E) 34 cm

Holt Physics: Light and Reflection
Sentence Completion

DIRECTIONS: For each question in this section, select the best answer from among the choices given and fill in the corresponding circle on the answer sheet.

13. The alignment of electromagnetic waves in such a way that the vibrations of the electric fields in each of the waves are parallel to each other is called _______.

    (A) incidence

    (B) reflection

    (C) linear polarization

    (D) destructive interference

    (E) constructive interference

14. Adding all three primary colors of light produces _______ light.

    (A) black

    (B) brown

    (C) colorless

    (D) cyan

    (E) magenta

15. Mixing all three primary pigments in equivalent proportions produces pigment that is _______.

    (A) black

    (B) brown

    (C) colorless

    (D) cyan

    (E) magenta

16. A mirror whose reflecting surface is a segment of the inside of a sphere is classified as _______.

    (A) concave

    (B) convex

    (C) flat

    (D) incidental

    (E) planar

Holt Physics: Light and Reflection
Reading Passage

The passage and table below are followed by questions based on their content. Answer the questions on the basis of what is <u>stated</u> or <u>implied</u> in the passage. For each question in this section, select the best answer from the choices given and fill in the corresponding circle on the answer sheet.

Questions 17–20 are based on the following passage and table.

While animals get the energy they need to survive from sugars found in food, plants get their energy through
Line photosynthesis, a biological process in
5 which the energy from sunlight is used to convert carbon dioxide and water into energy-providing sugars. An important part of this process is the absorption of sunlight by colorful pigments located in
10 the leaves of plants.

A pigment is a material that absorbs light of certain wavelengths and reflects light of other wavelengths. For example, a red pigment in paint absorbs all colors of
15 visible light except red. The pigment reflects red wavelengths of light, which causes the paint to appear red in color. In plants, the most dominant light-absorbing pigment is chlorophyll.
20 Chlorophyll most readily absorbs light of wavelengths in the ranges of 400–500 nm and 600–700 nm. Green light appears in the 495–570 nm range, which is in the range of wavelengths that are
25 reflected by chlorophyll. This is why most plants appear green in color—all other colors of visible light are absorbed and only green light is reflected by the plant.
30 Even though chlorophyll is the dominant photosynthesizing pigment in

plants, leaves contain many other pigments. These pigments reflect other colors of light, including yellow, orange,
35 and red. A colorful indication of their presence appears every autumn. In autumn, many plants lose their leaves as a result of the deterioration of leaf materials. This process is triggered by many factors,
40 including the change in temperature, as well as the change in the number of hours of available daylight. Different pigments breakdown at different rates. Thus, when the pigments that reflect green light
45 deteriorate, they no longer mask the pigments that reflect other colors of light. This means that some plants display other colors in their leaves for brief periods of time before losing their leaves entirely for
50 the season.

Wavelengths of Visible Light	
Violet	380–450 nm
Blue	450–495 nm
Green	495–570 nm
Yellow	570–590 nm
Orange	590–620 nm
Red	620–750 nm

GO ON TO THE NEXT PAGE

17. According to lines 11–19, pigments are

    (A) colored materials which can be found in paint

    (B) concave spherical mirrors

    (C) what allow plants to absorb oxygen

    (D) light waves of very long wavelengths

    (E) materials that absorb all colors of light

18. According to lines 20–29, what makes plants appear green?

    (A) a change in temperature

    (B) pigments that absorb green light

    (C) the reflection of light in the 495–570 nm range

    (D) a change in the number of hours of available daylight

    (E) pigments that reflect all colors of light but green

19. The word "deteriorate" in line 45 of the passage means

    (A) absorb

    (B) reflect

    (C) worsen

    (D) break down

    (E) become cheaper

20. According to lines 30–50, what change during autumn affects the color of leaves?

    (A) Green pigments are lost.

    (B) Green pigments are masked.

    (C) Green pigments are produced.

    (D) Red, orange, and yellow pigments are masked.

    (E) Red, orange, and yellow pigments are produced.

Holt Physics: Light and Reflection
Improving Sentences

DIRECTIONS: For each question in this section, select the best answer from among the choices given and fill in the corresponding circle on the answer sheet.

Part of each sentence in items 21 and 22 is underlined. Below each sentence are five ways of phrasing the underlined material. Choice A repeats the original phrasing; the other four choices are different. Choose the answer you think produces the most accurate sentence.

21. The law of reflection states that the incident and reflected angles of light <u>are equal</u>.

    (A) are equal

    (B) add up to 90°

    (C) add up to 180°

    (D) are related by a constant

    (E) are inverses of one another

22. The focal length, f, of a convex mirror is <u>twice the radius of curvature</u>.

    (A) twice the radius of curvature

    (B) half the image height

    (C) twice the magnification

    (D) always a positive number

    (E) always a negative number

Each sentence in items 23 and 24 contains either a single error or no error at all. If the sentence contains an error, choose the one underlined part that must be changed to make the sentence correct. If the sentence is correct, select choice E.

23. The <u>brightness</u> of light is <u>inversely</u>
          A   B
    proportional to the <u>square root</u> of the
                     C
    <u>distance</u> from the light source. <u>No error</u>
      D   E

24. <u>Flat</u> mirrors form <u>real</u> images that are
      A   B
    the same distance from the mirror's <u>surface</u>
                           C
    as the <u>object</u> is. <u>No error</u>
         D   E

Holt Physics: Refraction
Essay

DIRECTIONS: The essay gives you an opportunity to show how effectively you can develop and express ideas. You should, therefore, take care to develop your ideas, present concepts logically and clearly, and use language precisely.

Your essay must be written on your own paper. You may use both sides of a single sheet of notebook paper. You will have enough space if you write on every line, avoid wide margins, and keep your handwriting to a reasonable size. Remember that people who are not familiar with your handwriting will read what you write. Try to write or print so that what you are writing is legible to those readers.

IMPORTANT REMINDERS:
- **A pencil is required for the essay.** An essay written in ink will receive a score of zero.
- **Do not write your essay in your test book.** You will receive credit only for what you write on a single sheet of notebook paper.
- **An off-topic essay will receive a score of zero.**

Think carefully about the concept presented in the following passage and diagram and the assignment below.

The diagram below shows an ordinary metal spoon sitting in an ordinary glass of water.

ASSIGNMENT: What optical effect creates the illusion that this spoon is broken into two pieces? How do indices of refraction play a role? If the spoon were completely immersed, would it appear broken? Explain. Plan and write an essay in which you address these questions. Support your explanation with reasoning and examples taken from your reading, studies, experience, or observations.

Holt Physics: Refraction
Mathematics

DIRECTIONS: In this section, solve each problem using any available space on the page for scratch work. Then decide which of the choices given is best and fill in the corresponding circle on the answer sheet.

NOTES:
1. The use of a calculator is permitted. All numbers used are real numbers.
2. Figures that accompany problems in this test are intended to provide information useful in solving the problems. They are drawn as accurately as possible EXCEPT when it is stated in a specific problem that the figure is not drawn to scale. All figures lie in a plane unless otherwise indicated.

Reference Information

Wave Speed Equation

$c = f\lambda$

Index of Refraction

$n = \dfrac{c}{v}$

Thin-Lens Equation

$\dfrac{1}{p} + \dfrac{1}{q} = \dfrac{1}{f}$

Critical Angle

$\sin\theta_c = \dfrac{n_r}{n_i}$ for $n_i > n_r$

Speed of Light Traveling in a Vacuum

$c = 3.00 \times 10^8$ m/s

Snell's Law

$n_i \sin\theta_i = n_r \sin\theta_r$

Magnification of a Lens

$M = \dfrac{h'}{h} = -\dfrac{q}{p}$

Indices of Refraction, n

Air (at 0°C, 1 atm)	1.000 293
Carbon dioxide (at 0°C, 1 atm)	1.000 450
Glycerine (at 20°C)	1.473
Glass, flint (at 20°C)	1.66
Ice (at 0°C)	1.309
Water (at 20°C)	1.333

1. What is the angle of refraction for a ray of light that enters a fish tank full of water from air at an angle of 35.0° to the normal?

   (A) 25.5°

   (B) 26.3°

   (C) 43.0°

   (D) 46.6°

   (E) 49.7°

2. A ray of light traveling in water enters a transparent material. The incoming ray makes an angle of 30.0° with the normal, and the refracted ray makes an angle of 26.9° with the normal. What is the index of refraction of the transparent material?

   (A) 1.20

   (B) 1.31

   (C) 1.47

   (D) 1.49

   (E) 1.66

GO ON TO THE NEXT PAGE

| **Mathematics** *continued*

3. An object is placed 35.0 cm in front of a converging lens of focal length 15.0 cm. What is the image distance?

   (A) −50.0 cm

   (B) −20.0 cm

   (C) −10.5 cm

   (D) 10.5 cm

   (E) 26.2 cm

4. An object is placed 40.0 cm in front of a converging lens of focal length 10.0 cm. What is the magnification?

   (A) −13.3

   (B) −0.333

   (C) 0.0750

   (D) 0.333

   (E) 13.3

5. An object is placed 40.0 cm in front of a diverging lens of focal length 10.0 cm. What is the image distance?

   (A) −30.0 cm

   (B) −8.00 cm

   (C) 7.50 cm

   (D) 8.00 cm

   (E) 13.3 cm

6. A lens has a magnification of a 1.25. What is the image height of a 1.35 cm insect viewed through the lens?

   (A) 0.593 cm

   (B) 0.926 cm

   (C) 1.08 cm

   (D) 1.69 cm

   (E) 16.9 cm

7. What is the critical angle for light traveling from carbon dioxide into air?

   (A) 51.54076°

   (B) 88.98493°

   (C) 89.95437°

   (D) 99.98431°

   (E) 100.0157°

8. What is the critical angle for light traveling from flint glass into water?

   (A) 19.1°

   (B) 52.1°

   (C) 53.4°

   (D) 79.8°

   (E) 80.3°

GO ON TO THE NEXT PAGE

| Mathematics *continued*

Questions 9 and 10 are based on the following figure that shows light as it moves from one medium to another. (Figure not drawn to scale.)

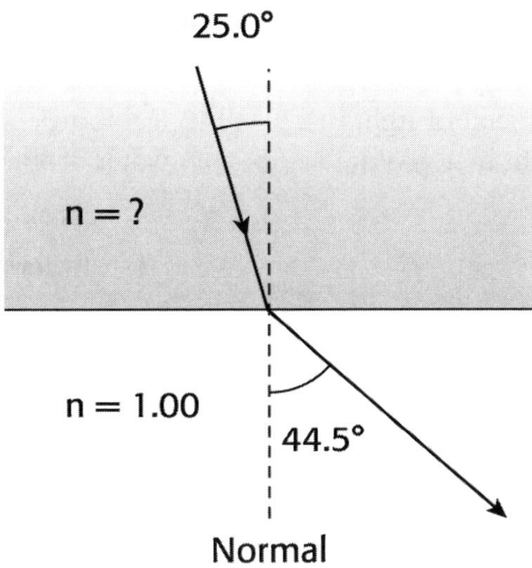

9. If the index of refraction of the bottom medium is approximately 1.00, what is the index of refraction for the top medium?

   (A) 1.31
   (B) 1.33
   (C) 1.47
   (D) 1.66
   (E) 1.78

10. What materials are most likely represented?

   (A) flint glass and air
   (B) water and air
   (C) water and ice
   (D) water and carbon dioxide
   (E) glycerine and carbon dioxide

Holt Physics: Refraction
Sentence Completion

DIRECTIONS: For each question in this section, select the best answer from among the choices given and fill in the corresponding circle on the answer sheet.

11. ________ is the ratio of the speed of light in a vacuum to the speed of light in a given transparent medium.

    (A) Chromatic aberration

    (B) Critical angle

    (C) Dispersion

    (D) Index of refraction

    (E) Total internal reflection

12. The focusing of different colors of light at different distances behind a lens is called ________.

    (A) chromatic aberration

    (B) critical angle

    (C) dispersion

    (D) index of refraction

    (E) total internal reflection

13. When light travels from one medium to the next at the ________, the refracted ray moves parallel to the boundary between the two media

    (A) chromatic aberration

    (B) critical angle

    (C) dispersion

    (D) index of refraction

    (E) normal

14. Rainbows are created by ________ of light in water droplets.

    (A) chromatic aberration

    (B) dispersion

    (C) reflection

    (D) spherical aberration

    (E) atmospheric refraction

15. According to Snell's law, as a light ray travels from one medium into another medium where its speed is different, the light ray will change its ________.

    (A) amplitude

    (B) direction

    (C) energy

    (D) frequency

    (E) wavelength

Holt Physics: Refraction
Reading Passages

The passages below are followed by questions based on their content; questions following a pair of related passages may also be based on the relationship between the paired passages. Answer the questions on the basis of what is <u>stated</u> or <u>implied</u> in the passages. For each question in this section, select the best answer from the choices given and fill in the corresponding circle on the answer sheet.

Questions 16–17 are based on the following passage.

    "How was swim practice?" called Kiki's mom from the car, where she sat fanning herself in the broiling heat. The twice-baked layer of air over the car's hood created ripple effects that made the car appear to have an invisible force field surrounding it. Boy, was it hot outside!

    Kiki sprinted from the poolside grass to the car. The blistering pavement scalded the delicate pads of her water-logged and prune-like feet. As they pulled out of the pool's parking lot, Kiki could see the shiny mirages—tricks of the light—that coated the sizzling concrete surfaces with a silvery liquid.

    "Let's go get snow cones," her mom said. And even the thought had a cooling effect on both of them.

(Line 5, 10, 15 in margin)

16. What physical factors could cause the effect described in lines 4–7?

  (A) a virtual image forming on the hot car

  (B) refraction of light through the swimming pool water

  (C) hot and cool air having different indices of refraction

  (D) pavement and air having different indices of refraction

  (E) movement of air from Kiki's mom's fan over the car's hood

17. In lines 13 and 14, the phrase "tricks of the light" refers to

  (A) hot concrete

  (B) silver liquids

  (C) lens aberrations

  (D) optical phenomena

  (E) total internal reflection

Questions 18–20 are based on the following passage.

    The human eye contains a lens that focuses light. However, the lens carries out mainly fine focusing of light. The majority of the refraction of light entering the eye takes place in the cornea, which has an index of refraction of 1.38. Air has an index of refraction of 1.00. The optics of the human eye rely on this difference in refractive power between the two media.

    When humans swim underwater without goggles or a mask, their corneas come into direct contact with water. Water has an index of refraction of 1.33. This value is so similar to that of the cornea that significantly less refraction occurs underwater than in air. Only when humans wear eyewear that create a layer of air between the water and the cornea is the normal refraction restored.

(Line 5, 10, 15, 20 in margin)

GO ON TO THE NEXT PAGE

Reading Passages *continued*

18. According to this passage, what is needed for a human to focus light coming into the eye?

    (A) a powerful lens

    (B) water surrounding the eye

    (C) a layer of air inside the eye

    (D) a material of low index of refraction in contact with the eye

    (E) a material of high index of refraction in contact with the eye

19. What does the term "eyewear" in line 18 of this passage most likely refer to?

    (A) contact lenses

    (B) eye makeup

    (C) eyeglasses

    (D) night vision goggles

    (E) swimming goggles

20. What other material, besides air, when surrounding the cornea could provide the difference in refractive power needed to focus light in the human eye? (Hint: Look at the list of indices of refraction at the beginning of this test.)

    (A) carbon dioxide

    (B) flint glass

    (C) glycerine

    (D) ice

    (E) water

Holt Physics: Refraction
Improving Sentences

DIRECTIONS: For each question in this section, select the best answer from among the choices given and fill in the corresponding circle on the answer sheet.

Part of each sentence in items 21 and 22 is underlined. Below each sentence are five ways of phrasing the underlined material. Choice A repeats the original phrasing; the other four choices are different. Choose the answer you think produces the most accurate sentence.

21. The image produced by a converging lens is <u>real and upright</u> when the object is outside the focal point.

    (A) real and upright

    (B) at infinity

    (C) virtual and upright

    (D) real and inverted

    (E) virtual and inverted

22. A negative sign for the magnification by a lens indicates that the image is <u>virtual and inverted</u>.

    (A) virtual and inverted

    (B) at infinity

    (C) real and upright

    (D) real and inverted

    (E) virtual and upright

Each sentence in items 23 and 24 contains either a single error or no error at all. If the sentence contains an error, choose the one underlined part that must be changed to make the sentence correct. If the sentence is correct, select choice E.

23. When light travels from a medium with a

    <u>lower</u> index of refraction to one with a
      A
    <u>higher</u> index of refraction, it is bent
      B
    <u>away from</u> the <u>normal</u>. <u>No error</u>
       C   D   E

24. <u>Total internal reflection</u> can occur when
          A
    <u>light</u> moves from a <u>material</u> with a higher
     B   C
    <u>chromatic aberration</u> to that with a lower
           D
    one. <u>No error</u>
        E

Holt Physics: Interference and Diffraction
Essay

DIRECTIONS: The essay gives you an opportunity to show how effectively you can develop and express ideas. You should, therefore, take care to develop your ideas, present concepts logically and clearly, and use language precisely.

Your essay must be written on your own paper. You may use both sides of a single sheet of notebook paper. You will have enough space if you write on every line, avoid wide margins, and keep your handwriting to a reasonable size. Remember that people who are not familiar with your handwriting will read what you write. Try to write or print so that what you are writing is legible to those readers.

IMPORTANT REMINDERS:
- **A pencil is required for the essay.** An essay written in ink will receive a score of zero.
- **Do not write your essay in your test book.** You will receive credit only for what you write on a single sheet of notebook paper.
- **An off-topic essay will receive a score of zero.**

Think carefully about the concept presented in the following passage and figures and the assignment below.

The figures below show three pairs of combining waves and the resulting waves that form when they combine.

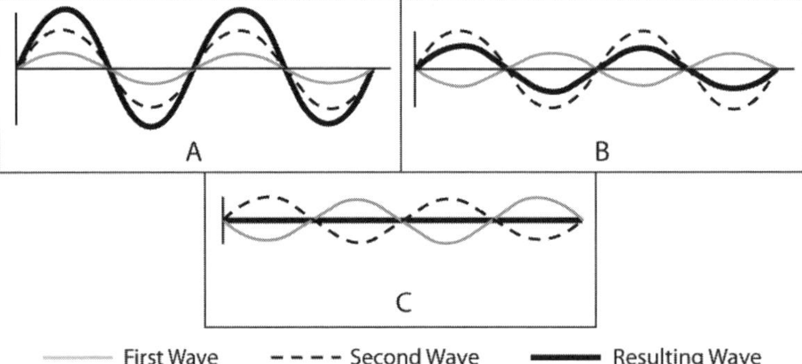

ASSIGNMENT: What types of interference are taking place in each of the three figures? In each case, how do the wavelength and amplitude of the resulting wave compare to the wavelengths and amplitudes of the two waves that combine to form it? How would light resulting from these types of interference appear? Plan and write an essay in which you address these questions. Support your explanation with reasoning and examples taken from your reading, studies, experience, or observations.

Holt Physics: Interference and Diffraction
Mathematics

DIRECTIONS: In this section, solve each problem using any available space on the page for scratch work. Then decide which of the choices given is best and fill in the corresponding circle on the answer sheet.

NOTES:
1. The use of a calculator is permitted. All numbers used are real numbers.
2. Figures that accompany problems in this test are intended to provide information useful in solving the problems. They are drawn as accurately as possible EXCEPT when it is stated in a specific problem that the figure is not drawn to scale. All figures lie in a plane unless otherwise indicated.

<table>
<tr><td>Wave Speed Equation
$c = f\lambda$</td><td>Speed of Light Traveling in a Vacuum
$c = 3.00 \times 10^8$ m/s</td></tr>
<tr><td>Equation for Constructive Interference
$d \sin\theta = \pm m\lambda \quad m = 0, 1, 2, 3, \ldots$</td><td>Equation for Destructive Interference
$d \sin\theta = \pm(m + \tfrac{1}{2})\lambda \quad m = 0, 1, 2, 3, \ldots$</td></tr>
</table>

(Reference Information)

Questions 1–3 are based on the following diagram of light falling on slits 0.020 mm apart producing a second-order bright fringe ($m = 2$) that measures $\theta = 3.50°$ from the central maximum. Note: Figure is not to scale.

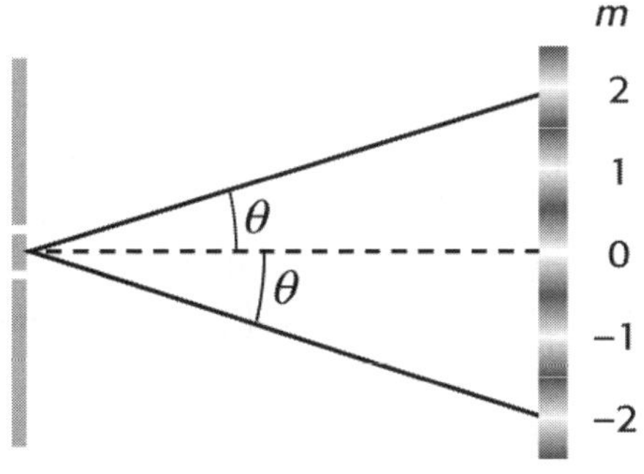

1. What is the wavelength of the light?

   (A) 1.2×10^{-6} m

   (B) 3.1×10^{-7} m

   (C) 4.5×10^{-7} m

   (D) 5.7×10^{-7} m

   (E) 6.1×10^{-7} m

2. What is the angle from the central maximum to the first bright fringe on either side of the central maximum?

   (A) 0.87°

   (B) 1.4°

   (C) 1.7°

   (D) 2.5°

   (E) 3.5°

3. What is the angle from the central maximum to the first dark fringe on either side of the central maximum?

   (A) 0.87°

   (B) 1.4°

   (C) 1.7°

   (D) 2.5°

   (E) 3.5°

GO ON TO THE NEXT PAGE

| **Mathematics** *continued*

4. Light falls on a double slit with slit separation of 3.35×10^{-6} m, and the first bright fringe is seen at an angle of $10.0°$ relative to the central maximum. What is the wavelength of the light?

   (A) 1.16×10^{-6} m

   (B) 1.45×10^{-7} m

   (C) 2.91×10^{-7} m

   (D) 3.35×10^{-7} m

   (E) 5.82×10^{-7} m

5. Given the information in the problem above, what is the angle from the central maximum to the second dark fringe on either side of the central maximum?

   (A) $10.1°$

   (B) $15.0°$

   (C) $15.1°$

   (D) $20.0°$

   (E) $20.3°$

6. The distance between two illuminated slits is 0.019 mm. The third-order bright fringe ($m = 3$) is measured at an angle of $5.55°$ from the central maximum. What is the wavelength of the light?

   (A) 5.5×10^{-6} m

   (C) 1.8×10^{-6} m

   (D) 5.7×10^{-7} m

   (D) 6.1×10^{-7} m

   (E) 6.4×10^{-7} m

7. Monochromatic light of wavelength 337.1 nm shines at a right angle to the surface of a diffraction grating that contains 5.0×10^5 lines/m. Find the angle at which the first-order maximum could be detected?

   (A) $1.7°$

   (B) $4.8°$

   (C) $4.9°$

   (D) $9.7°$

   (E) $19°$

8. White light shines through a diffraction grating with 12 500 lines/cm and projects a first-order spectrum on a viewing screen. At what angle does the first-order maximum for red light with a wavelength of 695 nm appear?

   (A) $0.996°$

   (B) $1.99°$

   (C) $30.2°$

   (D) $49.8°$

   (E) $60.3°$

9. A diffraction grating is calibrated by using the 435.8 nm line of a spectrum. The first-order maximum is found at an angle of $6.63°$. What is the number of lines per meter on this grating?

   (A) 2.65×10^3 lines/m

   (B) 3.77×10^4 lines/m

   (C) 2.65×10^5 lines/m

   (D) 5.30×10^5 lines/m

   (E) 1.89×10^6 lines/m

Holt Physics: Interference and Diffraction
Sentence Completion

DIRECTIONS: For each question in this section, select the best answer from among the choices given and fill in the corresponding circle on the answer sheet.

10. A _______ is a device that produces coherent light at a single wavelength.

    (A) diffraction grating

    (B) first-order maximum

    (C) fringe pattern

    (D) laser

    (E) prism

11. A device that consists of many equally spaced parallel slits is called a _______.

    (A) diffraction grating

    (B) first-order maximum

    (C) fringe pattern

    (D) laser

    (E) prism

12. Waves that are coherent have the same _______.

    (A) amplitude

    (B) energy

    (C) resolution

    (D) source

    (E) wavelength

13. In a microscope or telescope, resolving power depends on _______ and _______.

    (A) wave speed . . brightness

    (B) frequency . . source motion

    (C) wavelength . . aperture width

    (D) source motion . . observer location

    (E) diffraction grating . . fringe pattern

14. Light waves form a _______ by passing around an obstacle or bending through a slit and interfering with each other.

    (A) diffraction grating

    (B) diffraction pattern

    (C) electromagnetic spectrum

    (D) laser beam

    (E) resolving pattern

Holt Physics: Interference and Diffraction
Reading Passage

The passage below is followed by questions based on its content. Answer the questions on the basis of what is <u>stated</u> or <u>implied</u> in the passage. For each question in this section, select the best answer from the choices given and fill in the corresponding circle on the answer sheet.

Questions 15–20 are based on the following passage.

In 1887, the American physicists Albert Michelson and Edward Morley performed a famous demonstration that
Line debunked the once-popular notion of
5 "aether waves." Now known as the Michelson-Morley experiment, this important work ushered in the era of Albert Einstein and relativity.

In the 19th century, despite little
10 supportive experimental evidence, theorists held that light waves moved through an invisible medium called the aether. They theorized that light moved through aether in the same way that water
15 waves move across water and sound waves move through air. From this idea, scientists reasoned that the speed of light would be altered if the light source itself were also moving.

20 This change in the observed properties of a wave depending on its source's motion is in fact true of sound, which travels differently if its source is moving. You can demonstrate this effect
25 by listening to the radio in a car that drives by. When the car is moving toward you or away from you, music from the radio sounds very different than it would if the car were motionless. Wind can also
30 change the speed at which sound waves reach the ear of a stationary listener.

To study how light moved, Michelson

and Morley used an interferometer to split a beam of light and make the two beams
35 travel perpendicular to each other. An aether current moving with the Earth would speed or slow the light beam in one of the directions. A light interference, or fringe shift pattern, would change as the
40 scientists slowly rotated the interferometer, with first one and then the second light beam traveling in the direction of the aether flow.

The expected difference in the
45 measured speed of light, given the velocity of the Earth in its orbit around the sun, was about one hundredth of one percent of the speed of light. However, the fringe shift pattern did not exhibit any
50 measurable change.

15. According to lines 9–16, what was the theoretical aether thought to have in common with water and air?

(A) It is made up of atoms and molecules.

(B) It prevents the propagation of light waves.

(C) It is a medium through which waves can travel.

(D) When illuminated it is visible to the human eye.

(E) It was proven by Michelson and Morley to propagate light.

GO ON TO THE NEXT PAGE

Reading Passage *continued*

16. In line 5, the term "aether waves" refers to

    (A) light

    (B) sound

    (C) vacuum

    (D) water

    (E) wind

17. According to lines 20–31, what happens to sound waves when the source of the sound waves moves?

    (A) The sound waves create a wind that can be felt by nearby observers.

    (B) The sound waves appear to remain unchanged to a stationary observer.

    (C) The speed of sound can be altered if the source of the sound is moving.

    (D) The speed of sound does not change when the source of the sound moves.

    (E) The sound waves sound exactly like sound waves from a stationary source.

18. The passage implies that which two terms are synonyms?

    (A) "relativity" and "aether waves"

    (B) "relativity" and "light interference"

    (C) "interferometer" and "fringe shift pattern"

    (D) "light interference" and "fringe shift pattern"

    (E) "invisible medium" and "interferometer"

19. According to lines 32–50, what were the results of the Michelson-Morley experiment?

    (A) When light waves travel in the direction of aether flow, their speed increases.

    (B) Moving the light source changed the fringe shift pattern produced by the interferometer.

    (C) Moving the light source did not change the speed at which the emitted light waves traveled.

    (D) Using an interferometer splits a beam of light and makes the two beams travel perpendicular to each other.

    (E) They measured a difference of about one hundredth of one percent of the speed of light between the two waves.

20. Using the information in the passage, what conclusion can you draw about light?

    (A) In a vacuum, light travels at a speed of 3.00×10^8 m/s.

    (B) The speed of light can be altered if the source of the light is moving.

    (C) The speed of light does not change when the source of the light moves.

    (D) Light moves through aether in the same way that sound waves move through air.

    (E) Light moves through aether in the same way that water waves move across water.

Holt Physics: Interference and Diffraction
Improving Sentences

DIRECTIONS: For each question in this section, select the best answer from among the choices given and fill in the corresponding circle on the answer sheet.

Part of each sentence in items 21 and 22 is underlined. Below each sentence are five ways of phrasing the underlined material. Choice A repeats the original phrasing; the other four choices are different. Choose the answer you think produces the most accurate sentence.

21. In double-slit interference, the angle that determines where a bright fringe is located is related to <u>a whole number multiplied</u> by the wavelength.

    (A) a whole number multiplied

    (B) a fraction multiplied

    (C) an odd number divided

    (D) an odd number multiplied

    (E) an imaginary number divided

22. In a diffraction pattern that results from monochromatic light passing through a single slit, <u>only dark bands are formed</u>.

    (A) only dark bands are formed.

    (B) only bright bands are formed.

    (C) the bright bands that form are called maxima.

    (D) the bright bands that form are called minima.

    (E) the bright and dark bands that form have a random pattern.

Each sentence in items 23 and 24 contains either a single error or no error at all. If the sentence contains an error, choose the one underlined part that must be changed to make the sentence correct. If the sentence is correct, select choice E.

23. Light waves with the same <u>amplitude</u> and
                                            A

    <u>constant</u> phase differences <u>interfere</u> with
       B   C

    each other to produce light and dark

    <u>interference</u> patterns. <u>No error</u>
        D   E

24. <u>Incandescent</u> light is <u>coherent</u> because it
        A   B

    includes <u>light</u> of different <u>wavelengths</u>.
            C   D

    <u>No error</u>
     E

Holt Physics: Electric Forces and Fields
Essay

DIRECTIONS: The essay gives you an opportunity to show how effectively you can develop and express ideas. You should, therefore, take care to develop your ideas, present concepts logically and clearly, and use language precisely.

Your essay must be written on your own paper. You may use both sides of a single sheet of notebook paper. You will have enough space if you write on every line, avoid wide margins, and keep your handwriting to a reasonable size. Remember that people who are not familiar with your handwriting will read what you write. Try to write or print so that what you are writing is legible to those readers.

IMPORTANT REMINDERS:
- **A pencil is required for the essay.** An essay written in ink will receive a score of zero.
- **Do not write your essay in your test book.** You will receive credit only for what you write on a single sheet of notebook paper.
- **An off-topic essay will receive a score of zero.**

Think carefully about the concept presented in the following passage and diagrams and the assignment below.

Two balls are suspended by parallel strings so that they hang at the same level, as shown in the figures below

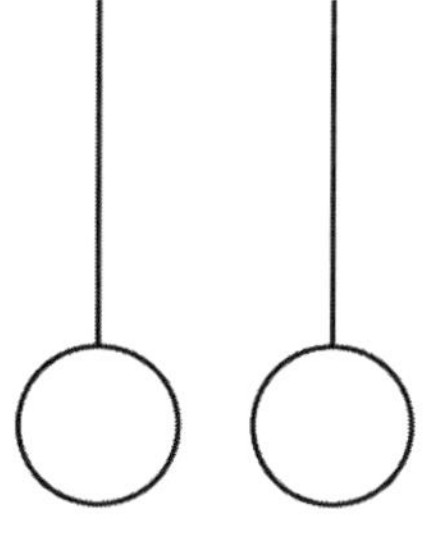 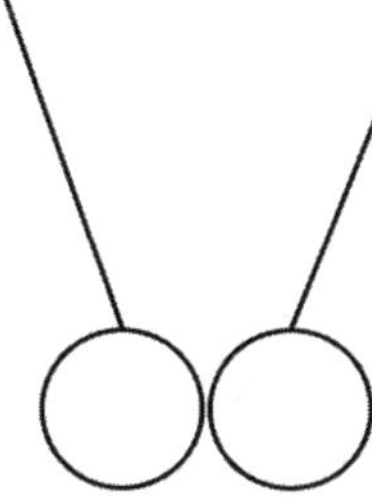 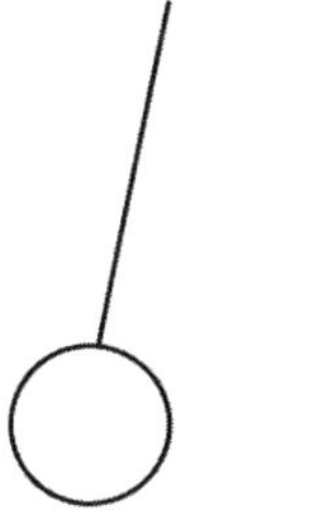

Figure A   Figure B   Figure C

ASSIGNMENT: What can you conclude about the electric charge on each of the balls in these figures? How do the figures demonstrate properties of electric charges? How might holding each of the balls at a greater distance apart affect them? Plan and write an essay in which you address these questions. Support your explanation with reasoning and examples taken from your reading, studies, experience, or observations.

Holt Physics: Electric Forces and Fields
Mathematics

DIRECTIONS: In this section, solve each problem using any available space on the page for scratch work. Then decide which of the choices given is best and fill in the corresponding circle on the answer sheet.

NOTES:
1. The use of a calculator is permitted. All numbers used are real numbers.
2. Figures that accompany problems in this test are intended to provide information useful in solving the problems. They are drawn as accurately as possible EXCEPT when it is stated in a specific problem that the figure is not drawn to scale. All figures lie in a plane unless otherwise indicated.

Reference Information

Coulomb's Law

$$F_{electric} = k_C \left(\frac{q_1 q_2}{r^2} \right)$$

$k_C = 8.99 \times 10^9 \text{ N} \bullet \text{m}^2$

$e = 1.602\,176 \times 10^{-19} \text{ C}$

$-1.0 \text{ C} = 6.2 \times 10^{18} \text{ electrons}$

Electric Field Strength due to Point Charge

$$E = k_C \frac{q}{r^2}$$

Cosine Function for Right Triangles

$$cos\,\theta = \frac{adj}{hyp}$$

Tangent Function for Right Triangles

$$tan\,\theta = \frac{opp}{adj}$$

Sine Function for Right Triangles

$$sin\,\theta = \frac{opp}{hyp}$$

1. How many electrons are there in -3.00 C of charge?

   (A) 6.02×10^{18} electrons

   (B) 6.24×10^{18} electrons

   (C) 1.60×10^{19} electrons

   (D) 1.86×10^{19} electrons

   (E) 4.81×10^{19} electrons

2. An object has a charge of $+2500e$. How many coulombs is this?

   (A) 1.6×10^{-19} C

   (B) 4.0×10^{-16} C

   (C) 2.5×10^3 C

   (D) 6.2×10^{18} C

   (E) 1.6×10^{22} C

GO ON TO THE NEXT PAGE

Mathematics *continued*

3. Two charged spheres are placed with their centers 0.15 m apart. One has a charge of $+25 \times 10^{-12}$ C and the other has a charge of -31×10^{-12} C. What is the electric force exerted on one sphere by the other?

   (A) 3.4×10^{-20} N

   (B) 4.6×10^{-11} N

   (C) 3.1×10^{-10} N

   (D) 2.4×10^{0} N

   (E) 2.2×10^{1} N

4. Two charged particles of $+5.0 \times 10^{-15}$ C and $+4.7 \times 10^{-15}$ C exert a repulsive force on each other of 350 N. What is the distance between the two charges?

   (A) 6.0×10^{-22} m

   (B) 2.5×10^{-11} m

   (C) 8.8×10^{-5} m

   (D) 4.1×10^{10} m

   (E) 1.7×10^{21} m

5. Three point charges, q_1, q_2, and q_3, lie along the x-axis at $x = 0$, $x = 2.0$ mm, and $x = 4.5$ mm, respectively. What is the magnitude and direction of the electric force on q_2 when $q_1 = +4.5$ µC, $q_2 = +3.0$ µC, and $q_3 = +6.0$ µC?

   (A) 4500 N toward the negative x-axis

   (B) 2600 N toward the positive x-axis

   (C) 3100 N toward the negative x-axis

   (D) 56000 N toward the negative x-axis

   (E) 56000 N toward the positive x-axis

6. Three charged particles are placed so that each particle is at the corner of a triangle that lies in the x-y plane. The charge at the origin is –3.0 µC, the charge at $x = 6.0$ cm on the x-axis is +4.0 µC, and the charge at $y = 4.0$ cm on the y-axis is +2.5 µC. What is the net electric force on the –3.0 µC charge?

   (A) 42 N, along the positive y-axis

   (B) 29 N, along the positive x-axis

   (C) 29 N, 55° below the positive x-axis

   (D) 42 N, 35° right of the positive x-axis

   (E) 52 N, 35° right of the positive x-axis

GO ON TO THE NEXT PAGE

| Mathematics *continued*

7. A charge q_1 of $+8.00 \times 10^{-9}$ C and a charge q_2 of $+4.00 \times 10^{-9}$ C are separated by a distance of 60.0 cm. What is the equilibrium position for a third charge of -25.0×10^{-9} C?

(A) 20.0 cm from q_1 (40.0 cm from q_2)

(B) 30.0 cm from q_1 (30.0 cm from q_2)

(C) 35.1 cm from q_1 (24.9 cm from q_2)

(D) 40.0 cm from q_1 (20.0 cm from q_2)

(E) 42.4 cm from q_1 (17.6 cm from q_2)

8. A charge q_1 of $+6.00 \times 10^{-9}$ C and a charge q_3 of -13.0×10^{-9} C are separated by a distance of 21.5 cm. If q_3 is at an equilibrium distance between q_1 and a third charge q_2 of $+5.50 \times 10^{-9}$ C, what is the distance between q_3 and q_2?

(A) 0.900 cm

(B) 4.24 cm

(C) 20.6 cm

(D) 42.1 cm

(E) 90.0 cm

9. A charge, $q_1 = 10.00$ μC, is located 25.0 cm from point A. What is the magnitude of the electric field at point A?

(A) 1.80×10^0 N/C

(B) 1.44×10^1 N/C

(C) 3.60×10^3 N/C

(D) 3.60×10^5 N/C

(E) 1.44×10^6 N/C

10. A charge, $q_1 = +7.00$ μC, is at the origin, and a second charge, $q_2 = -8.50$ μC, is on the x-axis 0.450 m from the origin. What is the electric field at a point on the y-axis 0.600 m from the origin?

(A) 8.16×10^4 N/C, 50.9° to the right of the positive y-axis

(B) 1.05×10^5 N/C, 50.9° to the right of the positive y-axis

(C) 1.09×10^5 N/C, 50.9° to the right of the positive y-axis

(D) 1.36×10^5 N/C, 50.9° to the right of the positive y-axis

(E) 1.75×10^5 N/C, 50.9° to the right of the positive y-axis

Holt Physics: Electric Forces and Fields
Sentence Completion

DIRECTIONS: For each question in this section, select the best answer from among the choices given and fill in the corresponding circle on the answer sheet.

11. A(n) ______ is a material in which charges cannot move freely.

    (A) electric field

    (B) electrical conductor

    (C) electrical insulator

    (D) induction

    (E) polarization

12. The process of charging a conductor by bringing it near another charged object and grounding the conductor is called ______.

    (A) conduction

    (B) electrification

    (C) electrostatic equilibrium

    (D) induction

    (E) polarization

13. Coulomb's law relates the magnitude of the electric force between two charges to the ______ and their ______.

    (A) sign of their charges . . masses

    (B) distance between them . . masses

    (C) distance between them . . product

    (D) difference in their masses . . sign

    (E) difference in their masses . . product

14. When an insulator is in the presence of a charged object, its molecules can experience a change in their centers of charge resulting in ______ of the insulator.

    (A) conduction

    (B) electrification

    (C) electrostatic equilibrium

    (D) induction

    (E) polarization

15. When no net motion of charge is occurring within a conductor, the conductor is said to be in ______.

    (A) conduction

    (B) electrification

    (C) electrostatic equilibrium

    (D) induction

    (E) polarization

Holt Physics: Electric Forces and Fields
Reading Passage

The passage below is followed by questions based on its content. Answer the questions on the basis of what is <u>stated</u> or <u>implied</u> in the passage. For each question in this section, select the best answer from the choices given and fill in the corresponding circle on the answer sheet.

Questions 16–20 are based on the following passage.

A new kind of lamp uses sulfur and microwaves to create light that is bright, energy-efficient, and looks a lot like

Line sunlight. In this sulfur lamp, the sulfur

5 bulb is flooded with microwave energy. In a microwave oven, an electric field creates microwave radiation that causes water and fat molecules to rotate and vibrate, which in turn increases the food's

10 temperature. In the sulfur lamp, the electric field accelerates electrons that strike sulfur molecules, causing them to become excited and emit light.

The sulfur lamp produces light of

15 great intensity. For example, light from two 3000 W microwave sulfur lamps can be routed through light pipes to illuminate an area 85 m wide. Because of its tremendous intensity, the lamp is not

20 practical for home use, says Michael Vry, vice president of research and development at Fusion Lighting, in Rockville, Maryland. "It certainly will not be in your kitchen until we can make a

25 lower-power version. So for the next few years, you'll find this being used in factories, and perhaps in sports arenas, aircraft hangars, and shopping malls, where the ceilings are high," says Vry.

30 However, the lamp cannot be used where the high temperature of overhead lighting is considered to be a negative factor, such

as in hockey rinks. But, adds Vry, "this is one of the few light sources with which

35 you can light plants to solar levels without cooking them."

Compared with other forms of outdoor lighting, the sulfur lamp makes it easier to discern a full spectrum of color.

40 For instance, if you are looking for your blue-green car in a parking lot at night, you may not recognize your car because the high-pressure sodium lamps used in most parking lots are deficient in the blue

45 and green frequency ranges, making your car look black. By contrast, says Vry, "The sulfur lamp spectrum contains all the colors. If we were to light up a parking lot with this light, you'd find your

50 car; you'd recognize its color."

Other advantages of the sulfur lamp are its high efficiency and reliability. A 1350 W sulfur lamp produces nearly six times as much light per watt as a 100 W

55 incandescent bulb. A sulfur light bulb is designed to last 60 000 hours, outlasting its microwave source, which usually has to be replaced between 15 000 and 20 000 hours.

GO ON TO THE NEXT PAGE

Reading Passage *continued*

16. According to lines 6–13, how is a sulfur lamp similar to a microwave oven?

    (A) Both use microwaves to heat food.

    (B) Both use microwaves to move particles.

    (C) Both produce light using excited sulfur molecules.

    (D) Both consume a lot of electricity in order to function.

    (E) Both are energy efficient machines that can be used in the kitchen.

17. According to lines 9–13, what accelerates the electrons that strike sulfur molecules in the sulfur lamp?

    (A) heat

    (B) protons

    (C) photons

    (D) an electric field

    (E) a positive charge

18. What does the phrase "negative factor" in line 32 most likely mean?

    (A) drawback

    (B) odd number

    (C) electric charge

    (D) boiling temperature

    (E) freezing temperature

19. According to lines 37–50, why is a sulfur lamp better than a sodium lamp for identifying the color of objects?

    (A) The sulfur lamp emits microwaves.

    (B) The sulfur lamp emits all colors of light.

    (C) The sodium lamp emits all colors of light.

    (D) The sulfur lamp emits only blue and green light.

    (E) The sodium lamp emits only blue and green light.

20. Which of the following is a drawback of using the sulfur lights described in this passage?

    (A) They melt ice.

    (B) They cook plants.

    (C) They have low intensity.

    (D) They are not energy efficient.

    (E) They cannot light large spaces.

Holt Physics: Electric Forces and Fields
Improving Sentences

DIRECTIONS: For each question in this section, select the best answer from among the choices given and fill in the corresponding circle on the answer sheet.

Part of each sentence in items 21 and 22 is underlined. Below each sentence are five ways of phrasing the underlined material. Choice A repeats the original phrasing; the other four choices are different. Choose the answer you think produces the most accurate sentence.

21. Electric field strength is stronger where the field lines are <u>far apart and weaker where they are close together</u>.

    (A) far apart and weaker where they are close together

    (B) not visible and weaker when they are visible

    (C) close together and weaker where they are far apart

    (D) crossing each other and weaker when they are not crossing

    (E) not crossing and weaker when they are crossing each other

22. The closer two charges are, <u>the more similar are the forces on them</u>.

    (A) the more similar are the forces on them

    (B) the greater is the force on them

    (C) the smaller is the force on them

    (D) the more positive is the force on them

    (E) the more negative is the force on them

Each sentence in items 23 and 24 contains either a single error or no error at all. If the sentence contains an error, choose the one underlined part that must be changed to make the sentence correct. If the sentence is correct, select choice E.

23. When an object becomes <u>polarized</u>, it has
    A
    <u>a</u> net charge but is <u>still able</u> to attract or
    B   C
    repel objects due to this <u>realignment</u> of
    D
    charge. <u>No error</u>
    E

24. <u>Two</u> <u>field lines</u> from the same <u>electric field</u>
    A   B   C
    <u>can</u> cross each other. <u>No error</u>
    D   E

Holt Physics: Electrical Energy and Current
Essay

DIRECTIONS: The essay gives you an opportunity to show how effectively you can develop and express ideas. You should, therefore, take care to develop your ideas, present concepts logically and clearly, and use language precisely.

Your essay must be written on your own paper. You may use both sides of a single sheet of notebook paper. You will have enough space if you write on every line, avoid wide margins, and keep your handwriting to a reasonable size. Remember that people who are not familiar with your handwriting will read what you write. Try to write or print so that what you are writing is legible to those readers.

IMPORTANT REMINDERS:
- **A pencil is required for the essay.** An essay written in ink will receive a score of zero.
- **Do not write your essay in your test book.** You will receive credit only for what you write on a single sheet of notebook paper.
- **An off-topic essay will receive a score of zero.**

Think carefully about the concept presented in the following graph and the assignment below.

The graph below shows the relationship between resistance and temperature.

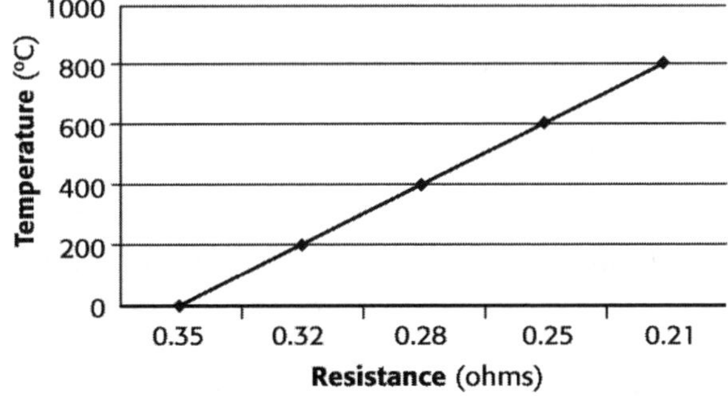

ASSIGNMENT: What is resistance? What is Ohm's law and what does it say about resistance? How is the resistance of a wire affected by factors such as temperature, length, cross-sectional area, and material? Plan and write an essay in which you address these questions. Support your explanation with reasoning and examples taken from your reading, studies, experience, or observations.

Holt Physics: Electrical Energy and Current
Mathematics

DIRECTIONS: In this section, solve each problem using any available space on the page for scratch work. Then decide which of the choices given is best and fill in the corresponding circle on the answer sheet.

NOTES:
1. The use of a calculator is permitted. All numbers used are real numbers.
2. Figures that accompany problems in this test are intended to provide information useful in solving the problems. They are drawn as accurately as possible EXCEPT when it is stated in a specific problem that the figure is not drawn to scale. All figures lie in a plane unless otherwise indicated.

Reference Information

Electrical and Potential Energy in a Uniform Electric Field
$$PE_{electric} = -qEd$$

Potential Difference in a Uniform Electric Field
$$\Delta V = -Ed$$

Capacitance
$$C = \frac{Q}{\Delta V}$$

Electrical Potential Energy Stored in a Charged Capacitor
$$PE_{electric} = \tfrac{1}{2}Q\Delta V$$

Resistance
$$R = \frac{\Delta V}{I}$$

Potential Difference
$$\Delta V = \frac{\Delta PE_{electric}}{q}$$

Potential Difference between a Point at Infinity and a Point near a Point Charge
$$\Delta V = k_C \frac{q}{r}$$

Capacitance for a Parallel-Plate Capacitor in a Vacuum
$$C = \varepsilon_0 \frac{A}{d}$$

Electric Current
$$I = \frac{\Delta Q}{\Delta t}$$

Electric Power
$$P = I\Delta V$$

---

1. A charge moves a distance of 15.0 cm in the direction of a uniform electric field whose magnitude is 195 N/C. As the charge moves, its electrical potential energy increases by 7.5×10^{-6} J. What is the charge on the moving particle?

   (A) -6.77×10^{-9} C

   (B) -2.56×10^{-7} C

   (C) -2.19×10^{-4} C

   (D) -4.56×10^{3} C

   (E) -1.73×10^{8} C

2. Producing an electric spark in a factory furnace requires an electric field of 9.5×10^{6} V/m. The gap between electrodes in the ignition device is 8.5 mm. What minimum potential difference must be supplied by the ignition device to start the furnace?

   (A) 1.2×10^{1} V

   (B) 8.1×10^{4} V

   (C) 6.5×10^{8} V

   (D) 1.1×10^{9} V

   (E) 8.9×10^{10} V

GO ON TO THE NEXT PAGE

Mathematics *continued*

3. A charge is released from rest in a uniform electric field with a magnitude of 4.5×10^3 V/m. The charge moves 350 cm as a result. What is the potential difference between the charge's initial and final positions?

   (A) 1.6×10^3 V

   (B) 4.2×10^3 V

   (C) 1.3×10^4 V

   (D) 6.3×10^4 V

   (E) 7.8×10^5 V

4. As a charged particle moves 8.0 m along an electric field of strength 950 N/C, its electrical potential energy decreases by 0.38 J. What is the particle's charge?

   (A) 5.0×10^{-5} C

   (B) 3.5×10^{-4} C

   (C) 2.9×10^{-4} C

   (D) 2.0×10^{-4} C

   (E) 2.0×10^{-2} C

5. A parallel-plate capacitor has a charge of 8.6 μC when charged by a potential difference of 3.5 V. What is its capacitance?

   (A) 5.0×10^{-6} F

   (B) 2.5×10^{-6} F

   (C) 4.1×10^{-5} F

   (D) 3.0×10^{-5} F

   (E) 3.4×10^{-4} F

6. A capacitor has a capacitance of 4.50 μF. What potential difference would be required to store 15.0 μC?

   (A) 0.0148 V

   (B) 0.300 V

   (C) 3.33 V

   (D) 10.5 V

   (E) 67.5 V

7. A capacitor has a capacitance of 1.50×10^{-10} F. How much charge is stored when the potential difference is 1.75 V?

   (A) 2.50×10^{-12} C

   (B) 8.57×10^{-11} C

   (C) 2.62×10^{-10} C

   (D) 1.17×10^{-10} C

   (E) 3.81×10^{-9} C

8. A total charge of 6.0×10^{-4} C passes through a cross-sectional area of a wire in 2.5 s. What is the current in the wire?

   (A) 2.4×10^{-4} A

   (B) 4.2×10^{-3} A

   (C) 1.5×10^{-3} A

   (D) 6.7×10^{-2} A

   (E) 2.4×10^{0} A

GO ON TO THE NEXT PAGE

Mathematics *continued*

9. If a wire carries a current of 1.35×10^{-3} mA, how long does it take for a charge of $7.36\ \mu C$ to pass a given cross-sectional area of the wire?

    (A) 0.00545 s

    (B) 0.101 s

    (C) 0.183 s

    (D) 5.45 s

    (E) 9.94 s

10. A 5.0 V battery is connected to a small electrical device with a resistance of $4.5\ \Omega$. What is the current in the electrical device?

    (A) 0.044 A

    (B) 0.50 A

    (C) 0.90 A

    (D) 1.1 A

    (E) 22 A

11. An electronic device is rated at 1.3 W when connected to 140 V. What is the resistance of this device?

    (A) $6.6 \times 10\text{--}5\ \Omega$

    (B) $9.3 \times 10\text{--}3\ \Omega$

    (C) $1.3 \times 100\ \Omega$

    (D) $1.8 \times 102\ \Omega$

    (E) $1.5 \times 104\ \Omega$

Holt Physics: Electrical Energy and Current
Sentence Completion

DIRECTIONS: For each question in this section, select the best answer from among the choices given and fill in the corresponding circle on the answer sheet.

12. The work that must be performed against electric forces to move a charge from a reference point to the point in question, divided by the charge, is the ______ at that point.

    (A) resistance

    (B) capacitance

    (C) electric current

    (D) electric potential

    (E) electrical potential energy

13. The ratio of charge to potential difference is ______.

    (A) resistance

    (B) capacitance

    (C) drift velocity

    (D) electric current

    (E) potential difference

14. The rate at which electric charges pass through a given area is called ______.

    (A) resistance

    (B) drift velocity

    (C) electric current

    (D) potential difference

    (E) electrical potential energy

15. Batteries convert ______ to electrical potential energy.

    (A) electric current

    (B) chemical energy

    (C) elastic potential energy

    (D) electrical mechanical energy

    (E) gravitational potential energy

Holt Physics: Electrical Energy and Current
Reading Passage

The passage below is followed by questions based on its content. Answer the questions on the basis of what is <u>stated</u> or <u>implied</u> in the passage. For each question in this section, select the best answer from the choices given and fill in the corresponding circle on the answer sheet.

Questions 16–20 are based on the following passage.

A diode is an electronic device that has an almost infinite resistance in one direction and nearly zero resistance in the other direction. Thus, a diode is able to
Line
5 pass current in only one direction, similar to the way a one-way valve passes water into a pipeline. The term *diode* comes from the Greek word parts *di-* ("two") and *hodos* ("way, path").

10 First developed in the late 1800s, the earliest diodes were either crystal diodes (solid state diodes) or vacuum tubes (gaseous state diodes). Most modern diodes are composed of two types of
15 semiconductors. They contain a p-n junction where the two types of semiconductors meet.

Diodes have a variety of uses in electrical systems. Devices called
20 "rectifiers" often use diodes to convert alternating current (AC) to direct current (DC). For example, some portable radios that normally run on batteries have power supplies, which are rectifiers that allow
25 you to plug the radio into an ordinary AC wall socket. Other uses of diodes include converting AM radio waves into signals that can be amplified to produce sound waves, measuring temperature, and
30 protecting delicate circuitry from high-voltage damage.

A colorful use of diodes is in the production of light. Light-emitting diodes, or LEDs, are semiconducting diodes that
35 act as tiny light sources in electronic devices. The color of light produced by an LED depends on the type of semiconductor used. For many purposes, LEDs are more energy efficient than traditional light bulbs, because they
40 produce more light with the same amount of power. You can find LEDs as indicator lights on dashboards and electrical panels, as infrared signal outputs on remote
45 controls, as bright arrays in traffic lights, and as tiny flashlights that can fit on a keychain.

16. According to lines 1–7, the side of a diode that has infinite resistance in one direction

(A) allows current to pass both ways

(B) is a stronger material than that of the other side

(C) is a weaker material than that of the other side

(D) stops current from passing back through it

(E) has the same electrical properties as the other side of the diode

GO ON TO THE NEXT PAGE

Reading Passage *continued*

---

17. Why might the Greek word parts for "diode," described in lines 7–9, be thought to convey the opposite of the word's meaning?

    (A) The earliest diodes were not made in Greece.

    (B) There are three main types of diodes, not only two.

    (C) A diode provides only one path, not two, for current to pass.

    (D) A diode has two sides made of two different materials, not one.

    (E) There are several materials that can be used to make a diode, not only two.

18. According to lines 10–17, what type of diode is most often found in modern electrical devices?

    (A) crystal diodes

    (B) gaseous state diodes

    (C) semiconductor diodes

    (D) solid state diodes

    (E) vacuum tubes

19. Lines 19–26 imply that

    (A) portable electronic devices can run only on AC

    (B) devices that use batteries are AC and wall sockets are DC

    (C) devices that use batteries are DC and wall sockets are AC

    (D) other countries have a different kind of AC than the United States

    (E) other countries have a different kind of DC than the United States

20. According to lines 32–47, how might a television's remote control use an LED?

    (A) to send signals across the room to the television using infrared light

    (B) to power the television with alternating current from a wall socket

    (C) to control the temperature of the television screen

    (D) to light up the television screen with many different colors

    (E) to save energy where an ordinary light bulb might use too much

---

Holt Physics: Electrical Energy and Current
Improving Sentences

DIRECTIONS: For each question in this section, select the best answer from among the choices given and fill in the corresponding circle on the answer sheet.

Part of each sentence in items 21 and 22 is underlined. Below each sentence are five ways of phrasing the underlined material. Choice A repeats the original phrasing; the other four choices are different. Choose the answer you think produces the most accurate sentence.

21. In direct current, charges move in <u>only one direction</u> with negative charges moving from a lower to higher electric potential.

    (A) only one direction

    (B) a spiral path

    (C) all directions

    (D) two directions

    (E) only straight lines

22. Ohmic materials have <u>little to no resistance</u>.

    (A) little to no resistance

    (B) a resistance that nears infinity

    (C) a tendency to deviate from Ohm's law

    (D) a constant current over a wide range of potential differences

    (E) a constant resistance over a wide range of potential differences

Each sentence in items 23 and 24 contains either a single error or no error at all. If the sentence contains an error, choose the one underlined part that must be changed to make the sentence correct. If the sentence is correct, select choice E.

23. According to <u>Ohm's law</u>, <u>potential</u>
              A   B
    difference and <u>current</u> are related by a
              C
    constant proportionality called <u>capacitance</u>.
                   D
    <u>No error</u>
     E

24. Because <u>resistance</u> <u>decreases</u> with <u>length</u>,
           A   B   C
    some <u>electrical energy</u> is lost when it is
           D
    transported by power lines over long

    distances. <u>No error</u>
           E

Holt Physics: Circuits and Circuit Elements
Essay

DIRECTIONS: The essay gives you an opportunity to show how effectively you can develop and express ideas. You should, therefore, take care to develop your ideas, present concepts logically and clearly, and use language precisely.

Your essay must be written on your own paper. You may use both sides of a single sheet of notebook paper. You will have enough space if you write on every line, avoid wide margins, and keep your handwriting to a reasonable size. Remember that people who are not familiar with your handwriting will read what you write. Try to write or print so that what you are writing is legible to those readers.

IMPORTANT REMINDERS

- **A pencil is required for the essay.** An essay written in ink will receive a score of zero.
- **Do not write your essay in your test book.** You will receive credit only for what you write on a single sheet of notebook paper.
- **An off-topic essay will receive a score of zero.**

Think carefully about the concept presented in the following diagrams and the assignment below.

The figures below show schematic diagrams for two different types of electric circuits.

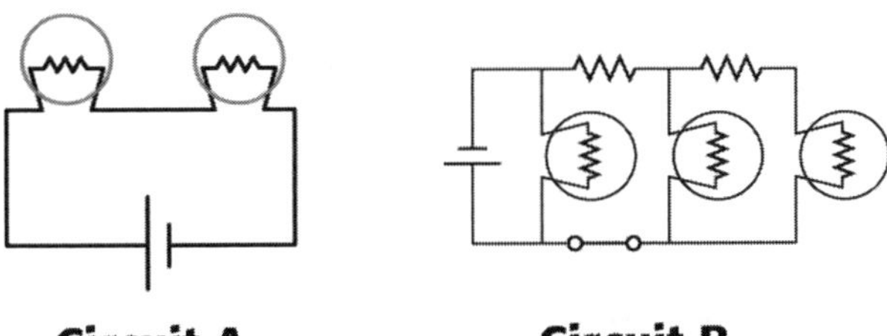

Circuit A   **Circuit B**

ASSIGNMENT: What kinds of components does each circuit have? How are these components connected (series or parallel)? How does the way they are connected affect the equivalent resistance of the circuit? How does the way they are connected affect the way the circuits conduct when one component is broken? Plan and write an essay in which you address these questions. Support your explanation with reasoning and examples taken from your reading, studies, experience, or observations.

Holt Physics: Circuits and Circuit Elements
Mathematics

DIRECTIONS: In this section, solve each problem using any available space on the page for scratch work. Then decide which of the choices given is best and fill in the corresponding circle on the answer sheet.

NOTES:
1. The use of a calculator is permitted. All numbers used are real numbers.
2. Figures that accompany problems in this test are intended to provide information useful in solving the problems. They are drawn as accurately as possible EXCEPT when it is stated in a specific problem that the figure is not drawn to scale. All figures lie in a plane unless otherwise indicated.

Reference Information

Resistors in Series

$$R_{eq} = R_1 + R_2 + R_3 \ldots$$

Resistance

$$R = \frac{\Delta V}{I}$$

Resistors in Parallel

$$\frac{1}{R_{eq}} = \frac{1}{R_1} + \frac{1}{R_2} + \frac{1}{R_3} \ldots$$

1. Two resistors, 2.50 Ω and 4.95 Ω, are wired in series to a 12.00 V battery. What is the equivalent resistance of the circuit?

   (A) 1.66 Ω

   (B) 2.45 Ω

   (C) 3.72 Ω

   (D) 7.45 Ω

   (E) 12.38 Ω

2. Two 3.5 Ω resistors and three 9.5 Ω resistors are connected in parallel. What is the equivalent resistance of the circuit?

   (A) 0.028 Ω

   (B) 0.89 Ω

   (C) 1.1 Ω

   (D) 2.6 Ω

   (E) 36 Ω

3. A 15.00 Ω resistor and 7.00 Ω resistor are connected in parallel to an emf source. A current of 1.50 A is in the 7.00 Ω resistor. What is the potential difference across the source?

   (A) 7.16 V

   (B) 10.5 V

   (C) 14.7 V

   (D) 16.5 V

   (E) 33.0 V

GO ON TO THE NEXT PAGE

Mathematics *continued*

4. Multiple light bulbs are connected in series across a 120.0 V source of emf. The current in the circuit is 1.25 A. If each light bulb has a resistance of 3.00 Ω, how many light bulbs are in the circuit?

   (A) 10 bulbs

   (B) 32 bulbs

   (C) 40 bulbs

   (D) 96 bulbs

   (E) 288 bulbs

Questions 5 and 6 are based on the following schematic diagram of a circuit with bulbs *A*, *B*, and *C*.

$R_A = 2.00\ \Omega$
$R_B = 4.00\ \Omega$
$R_C = 8.00\ \Omega$

5. What is the equivalent resistance of the circuit?

   (A) 0.0714 Ω

   (B) 0.875 Ω

   (C) 1.14 Ω

   (D) 4.67 Ω

   (E) 14.0 Ω

6. If the current in the circuit is 10.5 A, what is the potential difference across the source?

   (A) 0.750 V

   (B) 9.19 V

   (C) 12.0 V

   (D) 49.0 V

   (E) 147 V

Questions 7 and 8 are based on the following schematic diagram of a circuit with bulbs *A*, *B*, and *C*.

$R_A = 1.00\ \Omega$
$R_B = 5.00\ \Omega$
$R_C = 10.00\ \Omega$

7. What is the equivalent resistance of the circuit?

   (A) 0.0625 Ω

   (B) 0.769 Ω

   (C) 1.30 Ω

   (D) 5.30 Ω

   (E) 16.0 Ω

8. If the potential difference across bulb *B* is 3.5 V, what is the current in the circuit?

   (A) 0.22 A

   (B) 0.66 A

   (C) 0.70 A

   (D) 1.2 A

   (E) 3.5 A

GO ON TO THE NEXT PAGE

Mathematics *continued*

Questions 9 and 10 are based on the following schematic diagram of a circuit with bulbs *A*, *B*, and *C*.

$R_A = 2.00\ \Omega$
$R_B = 4.00\ \Omega$
$R_C = 8.00\ \Omega$

9. What is the equivalent resistance of the circuit?

   (A) 0.0714 Ω

   (B) 0.214 Ω

   (C) 0.875 Ω

   (D) 1.14 Ω

   (E) 4.67 Ω

10. If the current in bulb *B* is 8.50 A, what is the current in bulb *C*?

    (A) 2.83 A

    (B) 4.25 A

    (C) 8.50 A

    (D) 17.0 A

    (E) 39.7 A

Questions 11 and 12 are based on the following schematic diagram of a circuit with bulbs *A*, *B*, and *C*.

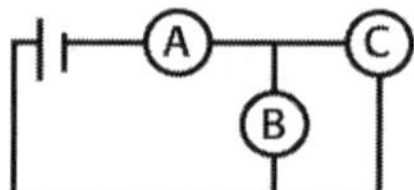

11. If the resistance of bulb *A* is 6 Ω, the resistance of bulb *B* is 18 Ω, and the equivalence resistance of the circuit is 12 Ω, what is the resistance of bulb *C*?

    (A) 0.0 Ω

    (B) 6.0 Ω

    (C) 7.2 Ω

    (D) 9.0 Ω

    (E) 18 Ω

12. If the potential difference across bulb *B* is 12.0 V, what is the potential difference across bulb *C*?

    (A) 3.0 V

    (B) 4.0 V

    (C) 6.0 V

    (D) 12.0 V

    (E) 24.0 V

Holt Physics: Circuits and Circuit Elements
Sentence Completion

DIRECTIONS: For each question in this section, select the best answer from among the choices given and fill in the corresponding circle on the answer sheet.

13. A _______ is a source of emf.

(A) battery

(B) conductor

(C) load

(D) resistor

(E) switch

14. Household circuits are arranged in parallel, so that appliances can all operate at the same _______.

(A) cost

(B) current

(C) energy consumption

(D) potential difference

(E) resistance

15. In a _______ circuit, the current is always the same for each resistor.

(A) closed

(B) electric

(C) open

(D) parallel

(E) series

16. The term _______ describes two or more components of a circuit that provide a single path for current.

(A) closed

(B) electric

(C) open

(D) parallel

(E) series

Holt Physics: Circuits and Circuit Elements
Reading Passage

The passage below is followed by questions based on its content. Answer the questions on the basis of what is <u>stated</u> or <u>implied</u> in the passage. For each question in this section, select the best answer from the choices given and fill in the corresponding circle on the answer sheet.

Questions 17–20 are based on the following passage.

"Heavy duty," "long-lasting alkaline," and "environmentally friendly rechargeable" are some of the labels that
Line manufacturers put on batteries. But how
5 do you know which one is the best?

The answer depends on how you will use it. Some batteries are used continuously, but others are turned off and on frequently, as in a stereo. Still
10 others must be able to hold a charge without being used, especially if they will be used in devices such as smoke detectors and flashlights.

In terms of price, "heavy duty"
15 batteries typically cost the least, but they last only about 30 percent as long as alkaline batteries. This makes them prohibitively expensive for most uses and makes them an unnecessary source of
20 landfill clutter.

Alkaline batteries are more expensive but have longer lives, lasting up to 6 h in continuous use and up to 18 h in intermittent use. They hold a full charge
25 for years, making them good for use in flashlights and similar devices. They are now less of an environmental problem because manufacturers stopped using mercury in such products several years
30 ago. However, because they are single-use batteries, they also end up in landfills very quickly.

Rechargeable cells are the most expensive to purchase initially. They can
35 cost up to $8, but if recycled, they are the most economical in the long-term and are the most environmentally sound choice. These cells, often called NiCads because they contain nickel (Ni) and cadmium
40 (Cd) metals, can be recharged hundreds of times. Although in some devices NiCads last only about half as long on one charge as alkaline batteries, the electricity to recharge them costs pennies.
45 NiCads lose about 1 percent of their stored energy each day they are not used and should therefore never be put in smoke detectors or flashlights.

17. What do lines 1–5 imply about the labels that manufacturers put on batteries?

(A) The terms used on these labels cannot always be trusted.

(B) "Heavy duty" batteries are the most environmentally friendly choice.

(C) Labels do not give information about the terminal voltage of the batteries.

(D) "Long-lasting alkaline" batteries are the least environmentally friendly choice.

(E) Labels give the best information about the uses of different types of batteries.

GO ON TO THE NEXT PAGE

Reading Passage *continued*

---

18. The smoke detector referred to in lines 9–13 is never turned off. What circuit component is therefore not needed in a smoke detector?

    (A) conductor

    (B) load

    (C) source of emf

    (D) switch

    (E) wire

19. Why are smoke detectors and flashlights singled out as electronic devices that require care when choosing a battery for them?

    (A) They are used to recharge cells.

    (B) They will never function with alkaline batteries.

    (C) They will never function with rechargeable batteries.

    (D) They use up "heavy duty" batteries faster than most other electronic devices.

    (E) They are devices that are used in emergencies, such as fires and power outages.

20. According to lines 33–48, what economical advantage over alkaline batteries makes up for the higher cost of rechargeable cells?

    (A) their smaller size when buried in a landfill

    (B) the low cost of recharging them and reusing them

    (C) the increased amount of time that they last with one charge

    (D) the decreased amount of time that they last with one charge

    (E) their reliability in safety devices such as smoke detectors and flashlights

Holt Physics: Circuits and Circuit Elements
Improving Sentences

DIRECTIONS: For each question in this section, select the best answer from among the choices given and fill in the corresponding circle on the answer sheet.

Part of each sentence in items 21 and 22 is underlined. Below each sentence are five ways of phrasing the underlined material. Choice A repeats the original phrasing; the other four choices are different. Choose the answer you think produces the most accurate sentence.

21. The equivalent resistance for a circuit with two resistors wired in parallel <u>is always less than</u> the smallest resistance in the group of resistors.

    (A) is always less than

    (B) always equals

    (C) is the reciprocal of

    (D) is always greater than

    (E) is the sum of the largest and

22. When resistors are wired in parallel, the potential difference across each resistor <u>is the reciprocal of the potential difference across the source</u>.

    (A) is the reciprocal of the potential difference across the source

    (B) equals the potential difference across the source

    (C) adds up to the total potential difference across the source

    (D) is the sum of the potential differences across all of the other resistors

    (E) is the reciprocal of the sum of the potential differences across the other resistors

Each sentence in items 23 and 24 contains either a single error or no error at all. If the sentence contains an error, choose the one underlined part that must be changed to make the sentence correct. If the sentence is correct, select choice E.

23. When <u>resistors</u> are connected in series, the
           A
    <u>potential difference</u> in each <u>resistor</u> is
           B   C
    <u>the same</u>. <u>No error</u>
         D   E

24. In a(n) <u>open circuit</u>, a <u>switch</u> is <u>closed</u>, and
           A   B   C
    the current is <u>zero</u>. <u>No error</u>
           D   E

Holt Physics: Magnetism
Essay

DIRECTIONS: **The essay gives you an opportunity to show how effectively you can develop and express ideas. You should, therefore, take care to develop your ideas, present concepts logically and clearly, and use language precisely.**

Your essay must be written on your own paper. You may use both sides of a single sheet of notebook paper. You will have enough space if you write on every line, avoid wide margins, and keep your handwriting to a reasonable size. Remember that people who are not familiar with your handwriting will read what you write. Try to write or print so that what you are writing is legible to those readers.

IMPORTANT REMINDERS:
- **A pencil is required for the essay.** An essay written in ink will receive a score of zero.
- **Do not write your essay in your test book.** You will receive credit only for what you write on a single sheet of notebook paper.
- **An off-topic essay will receive a score of zero.**

Think carefully about the concept presented in the following diagrams and the assignment below.

The diagrams below show the magnetic field lines that result when the poles of two magnets meet north to south and north to north.

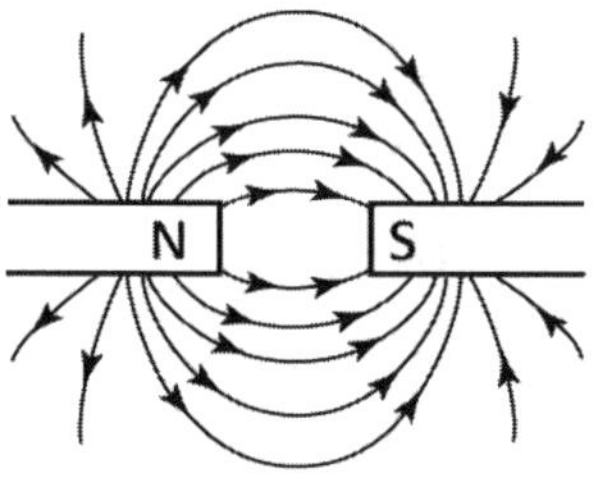

Figure A

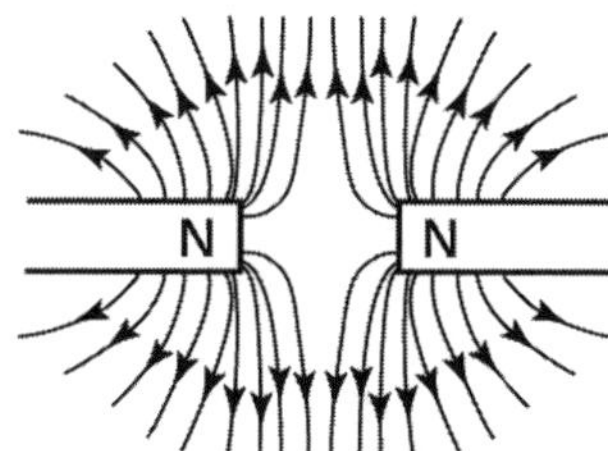

Figure B

ASSIGNMENT: **What happens when two magnets meet at like poles and when two magnets meet at opposite poles? What is a magnetic field? How do the magnetic field lines shown above relate to the behavior of the magnets in each situation? Plan and write an essay in which you address these questions. Support your explanation with reasoning and examples taken from your reading, studies, experience, or observations.**

Holt Physics: Magnetism
Mathematics

DIRECTIONS: In this section, solve each problem using any available space on the page for scratch work. Then decide which of the choices given is best and fill in the corresponding circle on the answer sheet.

NOTES:
1. The use of a calculator is permitted. All numbers used are real numbers.
2. Figures that accompany problems in this test are intended to provide information useful in solving the problems. They are drawn as accurately as possible EXCEPT when it is stated in a specific problem that the figure is not drawn to scale. All figures lie in a plane unless otherwise indicated.

Reference Information

Magnitude of a Magnetic Field

$$B = \frac{F_{magnetic}}{qv}$$

Force on a Current-Carrying Conductor Perpendicular to a Magnetic Field

$$F_{magnetic} = BI\ell$$

1. A positive charge of 1.8 μC experiences a force of 9.5×10^{-10} N due to a magnetic field. The field has a magnitude of 3.5×10^{-5} T. What is the speed of the charge?

   (A) 4.9×10^{-11} m/s

   (B) 1.8×10^{-8} m/s

   (C) 6.6×10^{-2} m/s

   (D) 1.5×10^{1} m/s

   (E) 2.0×10^{10} m/s

2. If -3.3×10^{-11} C charge experiences a force of 5.0×10^{-12} N while traveling in a magnetic field of 9.5 cT, what is its speed?

   (A) 0.014 m/s

   (B) 0.63 m/s

   (C) 1.6 m/s

   (D) 6.6 m/s

   (E) 69 m/s

3. A proton (1.60×10^{-19} C) moves normal to a magnetic field of 1.98×10^{-3} T. What is the speed of the proton if the magnitude of the magnetic force on it is 3.90×10^{-16} N?

   (A) 3.15×10^{7} m/s

   (B) 8.12×10^{7} m/s

   (C) 1.23×10^{6} m/s

   (D) 3.17×10^{7} m/s

   (E) 1.61×10^{8} m/s

4. If a negative charge of 2.9×10^{-17} C moves with a speed of 4.0×10^{5} m/s through a 1.7 T magnetic field, what force will act on it?

   (A) 1.4×10^{-12} N

   (B) 6.8×10^{-12} N

   (C) 1.5×10^{-11} N

   (D) 2.0×10^{-11} N

   (E) 5.1×10^{-10} N

GO ON TO THE NEXT PAGE

Mathematics *continued*

5. An electron (-1.6×10^{-19} C) experiences a force of 3.5×10^{-17} N as it moves with a speed of 4.0×10^{6} m/s through a magnetic field. What is the magnitude of the magnetic field?

   (A) 1.8×10^{-4} T

   (B) 5.5×10^{-5} T

   (C) 2.4×10^{-12} T

   (D) 4.5×10^{-28} T

   (E) 2.2×10^{-29} T

6. A 24.5 m wire carries a current of 15.0 A. If the magnetic force on the wire due to a magnetic field has a magnitude of 5.50×10^{-3} N, what is the magnitude of the magnetic field at this location?

   (A) 1.50×10^{-5} T

   (B) 6.68×10^{-4} T

   (C) 3.37×10^{-3} T

   (D) 4.95×10^{-1} T

   (E) 2.02×10^{0} T

7. A wire 650 cm long carries a current of 9.0 A. A magnetic force of 5.0×10^{-4} N acts on the wire. What is the magnitude of the magnetic field producing the force?

   (A) 8.5×10^{-8} T

   (B) 4.3×10^{-7} T

   (C) 8.5×10^{-6} T

   (D) 1.2×10^{-5} T

   (E) 2.3×10^{-2} T

8. A length of wire carries a current of 28.0 A. If the magnetic force on the wire due to a 9.7×10^{-3} T magnetic field has a magnitude of 1.2 N, how long is the wire?

   (A) 0.23 m

   (B) 0.33 m

   (C) 0.44 m

   (D) 3.1 m

   (E) 4.4 m

9. A 95 cm wire experiences a uniform magnetic field of magnitude 0.85 T. If the wire carries a current of 16.5 A, what is the magnitude of the magnetic force produced by the field?

   (A) 0.054 N

   (B) 0.075 N

   (C) 1.4 N

   (D) 13 N

   (E) 18 N

10. The magnetic force acting on a wire due to a 1.1 T uniform magnetic field is 3.8 N. If the current in the wire is 8.0 A, what is the length of the wire that is inside the magnetic field?

    (A) 0.29 cm

    (B) 2.3 cm

    (C) 3.0 cm

    (D) 33 cm

    (E) 43 cm

Holt Physics: Magnetism
Sentence Completion

DIRECTIONS: For each question in this section, select the best answer from among the choices given and fill in the corresponding circle on the answer sheet.

11. A magnetic _______ is a group of atoms whose magnetic fields are aligned.

    (A) declination

    (B) domain

    (C) field

    (D) flux

    (E) pole

12. A magnetic _______ is a region in which a magnetic force can be detected.

    (A) declination

    (B) domain

    (C) field

    (D) flux

    (E) pole

13. Magnetic _______ is the number of field lines that cross a certain area at right angles to that area.

    (A) declination

    (B) domain

    (C) field

    (D) flux

    (E) pole

14. A _______ produces a strong magnetic field by combining several loops of insulated wire.

    (A) ammeter

    (B) galvanometer

    (C) magnet

    (D) solenoid

    (E) voltmeter

15. The magnetic north pole of Earth corresponds to the _______, and the magnetic south pole corresponds to the _______.

    (A) geographic West . . geographic East

    (B) geographic poles. . geographic equator

    (C) geographic equator . . geographic poles

    (D) geographic South Pole . . geographic North Pole

    (E) geographic North Pole . . geographic South Pole

Holt Physics: Magnetism
Reading Passages

The passages below are followed by questions based on their content; questions following a pair of related passages may also be based on the relationship between the paired passages. Answer the questions on the basis of what is <u>stated</u> or <u>implied</u> in the passages. For each question in this section, select the best answer from the choices given and fill in the corresponding circle on the answer sheet.

Questions 16–17 are based on the following passage.

Magnetite, or lodestone, is a naturally occurring mineral that has magnetic properties. Scientists hypothesize that some animals, and perhaps even people,
Line
5   have a sixth sense—magnetoception—that results from natural crystals of magnetite found in their heads. Some bacteria, pigeons, turtles, and honeybees are known to have tiny deposits of the
10   magnetite crystals that may help these creatures navigate by allowing them to sense Earth's magnetic field.

Studies have shown that migratory birds can get lost when trying to find their
15   way through regions where the Earth's magnetic field is disrupted by large iron deposits. Many scientists suspect that the disorientation of these birds results from their confused sense of magnetoception.

16. How do scientists predict animals use the magnetite crystals described in lines 3–7?

(A) to process iron in their diets

(B) to detect large iron deposits

(C) to sense what others are thinking

(D) to find their way when they travel

(E) to attract iron-containing minerals

17. The passage implies that some animals can detect the orientation of

(A) a magnetic field

(B) any metal object

(C) negative charges

(D) magnetic crystals

(E) any iron-containing object

Questions 18–20 are based on the following passage.

Some of the most powerful magnets commercially available are neodymium magnets. Often plated in nickel to prevent
Line   shattering, these fragile magnets are made
5   up of the elements iron, boron, and neodymium. In spite of their brittleness, some neodymium magnets are so powerful that their magnetic force can lift objects that are over 1000 times their
10   mass. They can be found in computer hard drives, loudspeakers, and some toys.

While their strength can be useful, it can also be dangerous. When handled without care, large neodymium magnets
15   can pull nearby steel- and iron-containing objects toward them at dangerous speeds, possibly injuring someone standing in the way. Also, the magnets are so strong that two brought near one another can snap
20   together with such a force that they can pierce skin or break bones.

GO ON TO THE NEXT PAGE

Reading Passages *continued*

18. According to lines 1–10, why are neodymium magnets often plated in nickel?

    (A) to make them more attractive

    (B) to prevent them from breaking

    (C) to prevent them from attracting metals

    (D) to ensure that users do not break bones

    (E) to ensure that users are not poisoned by them

19. What does the word "powerful" in line 1 most likely mean?

    (A) influential

    (B) physically strong

    (C) able to endure collisions

    (D) producing a strong magnetic force

    (E) holding up to physical wear and tear

20. According to lines 12–21, why might it be dangerous to handle a neodymium magnet near a small steel object?

    (A) The magnet might shatter, which could produce sharp pieces.

    (B) The magnet could disorient people who can sense magnetic fields.

    (C) Some of the poisonous materials in the magnet could rub off on the skin.

    (D) The magnet might attract the object toward it, harming any body part that is in the way.

    (E) The magnet might attract the object toward it, causing it to break and produce sharp pieces.

Holt Physics: Magnetism
Improving Sentences

DIRECTIONS: For each question in this section, select the best answer from among the choices given and fill in the corresponding circle on the answer sheet.

Part of each sentence in items 21 and 22 is underlined. Below each sentence are five ways of phrasing the underlined material. Choice A repeats the original phrasing; the other four choices are different. Choose the answer you think produces the most accurate sentence.

21. Soft magnetic materials are <u>not ferromagnetic</u>.

    (A) not ferromagnetic

    (B) easily magnetized, but tend to lose their magnetism easily

    (C) difficult to magnetize, and tend to lose their magnetism easily

    (D) easily magnetized, and once magnetized, tend to retain their magnetism

    (E) difficult to magnetize, but once magnetized, tend to retain their magnetism

22. When a charged particle moves through a uniform magnetic field with an initial velocity exactly perpendicular to the field, the particle <u>follows a spiral path</u>.

    (A) follows a spiral path

    (B) follows a helical path

    (C) follows a circular path

    (D) moves in a zigzag line

    (E) moves in a straight line

Each sentence in items 23 and 24 contains either a single error or no error at all. If the sentence contains an error, choose the one underlined part that must be changed to make the sentence correct. If the sentence is correct, select choice E.

23. A(n) <u>looped</u>, current-carrying wire has a
    A
    <u>cylindrical</u> magnetic field with magnetic
    B
    field lines that form <u>concentric circles</u>
    C
    <u>around</u> the wire. <u>No error</u>
    D   E

24. The difference between <u>true north</u>, which is
    A
    defined by the <u>axis of rotation</u> of Earth, and
    B
    north indicated by a <u>compass</u> is referred to
    C
    as <u>magnetic flux</u>. <u>No error</u>
    D   E

Holt Physics: Electromagnetic Induction
Essay

DIRECTIONS: The essay gives you an opportunity to show how effectively you can develop and express ideas. You should, therefore, take care to develop your ideas, present concepts logically and clearly, and use language precisely.

Your essay must be written on your own paper. You may use both sides of a single sheet of notebook paper. You will have enough space if you write on every line, avoid wide margins, and keep your handwriting to a reasonable size. Remember that people who are not familiar with your handwriting will read what you write. Try to write or print so that what you are writing is legible to those readers.

IMPORTANT REMINDERS:

- **A pencil is required for the essay.** An essay written in ink will receive a score of zero.
- **Do not write your essay in your test book.** You will receive credit only for what you write on a single sheet of notebook paper.
- **An off-topic essay will receive a score of zero.**

Think carefully about the concept presented in the following diagram and the assignment below.

The diagram below shows an ordinary bar magnet and a coil of wire. The magnet can move from side to side as shown.

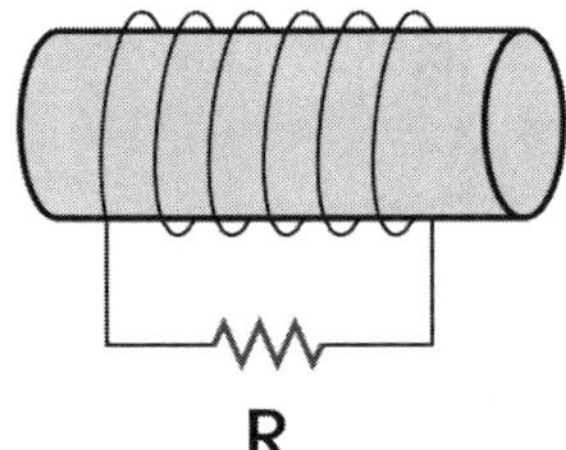

ASSIGNMENT: What does moving the magnet to the right do to the current in the wire? What does moving the magnet to the left do to the current in the wire? What is this process called? What happens when the magnet does not move? Plan and write an essay in which you address these questions. Support your explanation with reasoning and examples taken from your reading, studies, experience, or observations.

Mathematics

DIRECTIONS: In this section, solve each problem using any available space on the page for scratch work. Then decide which of the choices given is best and fill in the corresponding circle on the answer sheet.

NOTES:
1. The use of a calculator is permitted. All numbers used are real numbers.
2. Figures that accompany problems in this test are intended to provide information useful in solving the problems. They are drawn as accurately as possible EXCEPT when it is stated in a specific problem that the figure is not drawn to scale. All figures lie in a plane unless otherwise indicated.

Reference Information

Faraday's Law of Magnetic Induction	**Magnetic Flux**
$\text{emf} = -N\dfrac{\Delta\Phi M}{\Delta t}$	$\Phi_M = AB\cos\theta$
rms Value for Potential Difference	**rms Value for Current**
$\Delta V_{rms} = \dfrac{\Delta V_{max}}{\sqrt{2}}$	$I_{rms} = \dfrac{I_{max}}{\sqrt{2}}$
Transformer Equation	**Resistance**
$\Delta V_2 = \dfrac{N_2}{N_1}\Delta V_1$	$R = \dfrac{\Delta V}{I}$
Area of a Circle	
$A = \pi r^2$	

1. A single circular loop with a radius of 8.75 cm is placed in a uniform external magnetic field with a strength of 8.3×10^{-2} T so that the plane of the loop is perpendicular to the field. The loop is pulled steadily out of the field in 0.15 s. What is the average induced emf during this interval?

   (A) 0.013 mV

   (B) 6.7 mV

   (C) 13 mV

   (D) 27 mV

   (E) 48 mV

2. A coil with 145 turns of wire, a total resistance of 15 Ω, and a cross-sectional area of 0.50 m^2 is positioned with its plane perpendicular to the field of a powerful electromagnet. What average current is induced in the coil during the 0.25 s that the magnetic field drops from 1.20 T to 0.60 T?

   (A) 12 A

   (B) 18 A

   (C) 23 A

   (D) 36 A

   (E) 170 A

GO ON TO THE NEXT PAGE

Mathematics *continued*

3. A 615-turn circular-loop coil with a diameter of 24.5 cm is placed in a uniform external magnetic field so that the plane of the coil is perpendicular to the field. The coil is pulled steadily out of the field in 50.5 ms. If an average emf of 2.04 V is induced in the coil, what is the value of the magnetic field?

   (A) 3.42×10^{-4} T

   (B) 6.84×10^{-4} T

   (C) 1.17×10^{-3} T

   (D) 1.37×10^{-3} T

   (E) 3.56×10^{-3} T

4. What is the rms current in a resistor that has a resistance of 35 Ω and an rms emf of 95 V?

   (A) 0.37 A

   (B) 2.7 A

   (C) 60 A

   (D) 130 A

   (E) 3300 A

5. The largest emf that can be placed across a certain load at any instant is 955 V. What is the largest rms emf that can be placed across the load without damaging it?

   (A) 30.9 V

   (B) 478 V

   (C) 675 V

   (D) 1350 V

   (E) 1910 V

6. An electrical appliance is plugged into a source of alternating emf with an rms value of 125 V. A resistor in the appliance is designed to convey a current with a peak value of 15.5 A. What is the resistance of the resistor?

   (A) 80.6 Ω

   (B) 11.4 Ω

   (C) 16.1 Ω

   (D) 31.8 Ω

   (E) 1370 Ω

7. A generator with a maximum output emf of 150 V is connected to a 35 Ω resistor. What is the rms potential difference?

   (A) 2.1 V

   (B) 3.0 V

   (C) 4.3 V

   (D) 12 V

   (E) 110 V

8. A step-up transformer is used to increase emf from 155 V to 1700 V. If the primary has 110 turns, how many turns must the secondary have?

   (A) 10 turns

   (B) 15 turns

   (C) 500 turns

   (D) 1200 turns

   (E) 2400 turns

GO ON TO THE NEXT PAGE

Mathematics *continued*

9. A step-down transformer is supposed to decrease potential difference from 9.0 V to 2.5 V. If the number of turns in the secondary is 50, what is the number of turns needed in the primary?

   (A) 14 turns

   (B) 25 turns

   (C) 180 turns

   (D) 200 turns

   (E) 1100 turns

10. An electrical engineer builds a step-up transformer that has 450 turns in its primary and 1600 turns in its secondary. If the potential difference across the primary is 395 V, what is the potential difference across the secondary?

   (A) 110 V

   (B) 1200 V

   (C) 1400 V

   (D) 1800 V

   (E) 1900 V

Holt Physics: Electromagnetic Induction
Sentence Completion

DIRECTIONS: For each question in this section, select the best answer from among the choices given and fill in the corresponding circle on the answer sheet.

11. The process of creating a current in a circuit loop by changing the magnetic flux in the loop is called ______.

    (A) alternating current

    (B) electromagnetic induction

    (C) electromagnetic radiation

    (D) mutual inductance

    (E) rms current

12. The ability of one circuit to induce an emf in a nearby circuit in the presence of a changing current is called ______.

    (A) alternating current

    (B) back emf

    (C) electromagnetic induction

    (D) mutual inductance

    (E) rms current

13. The ______ induced in a motor's coil tends to reduce the current in the coil of the motor.

    (A) alternating current

    (B) back emf

    (C) direct current

    (D) mutual inductance

    (E) rms current

14. According to ______, the average induced emf in a circuit is equal to the number of loops in the circuit multiplied by the time rate of change of the magnetic flux.

    (A) Coulomb's law

    (B) Faraday's law of induction

    (C) inverse-square law

    (D) Lenz's law

    (E) Plank's constant

15. A ______ is a device that increases the emf of alternating current.

    (A) electromagnet

    (B) generator

    (C) motor

    (D) step-down transformer

    (E) step-up transformer

Holt Physics: Electromagnetic Induction
Reading Passages

**The passages below are followed by questions based on their content; questions
following a pair of related passages may also be based on the relationship between
the paired passages. Answer the questions on the basis of what is <u>stated</u> or <u>implied</u>
in the passages. For each question in this section, select the best answer from the
choices given and fill in the corresponding circle on the answer sheet.**

**Questions 16–20 are based on the following
passages.**

Passage 1

    After New Zealand chemist Ernest
Rutherford discovered the proton in 1911,
the British physicist Henry Moseley
(1887–1915) exposed several elements to
a beam of electrons, causing the samples
to emit X rays. With his experimental
results, he derived a relationship between
emitted X-ray frequency and the number
of protons in an atom.

    In 1913, Moseley created a periodic
table of the elements that updated the
table produced by Dmitri Mendeleev in
1869, which ordered elements by their
atomic masses. Moseley's work showed
that proton number was a measurable
quantity that could be used instead of
atomic mass to predict element properties.

Passage 2

    Black holes are celestial objects so
massive that even light does not move
fast enough to escape their gravity.
Although the existence of black holes has
been theoretically suggested, no black
hole has been conclusively discovered.
Nevertheless, numerous observations
have provided evidence of their existence.

    Astronomers have observed
tremendous amounts of X rays and other
radiation coming from regions that are
near visible stars, although no stars
appear to be the source of the radiation. If
the visible star has a black hole as a
companion, it could be losing some of its
outer atmospheric gases to the black hole,
and those atmospheric gases could be
emitting radiation as they accelerate
closer to the black hole.

    The large amount of energy that
galactic centers produce suggests to many
astrophysicists that the energy sources are
super-massive black holes. The galaxy
NGC 4261 is likely to have a black hole
at its center. Some astronomers reason
that the Milky Way, our own galaxy,
contains a black hole about the size of our
solar system.

16. According to lines 1–9 of Passage 1, what
was the dependent variable in Moseley's
experiment?

    (A) the mass of the proton

    (B) the number of X rays

    (C) the frequency of the X ray

    (D) the atomic mass of the element

    (E) the mass of the elemental sample

GO ON TO THE NEXT PAGE

17. According to Passage 1, if number of protons determines the identity of an element, how did Moseley's experiment change the way that scientists could identify elements?

    (A) After Moseley, scientists could look at atomic mass to identify elements.

    (B) After Moseley, scientists could look at X-ray intensity to identify elements.

    (C) After Moseley, scientists could look at the number of electrons to identify elements.

    (D) After Moseley, scientists could look at the emitted X-ray frequency to identify elements.

    (E) After Moseley, scientists could look at the visible color of a sample to identify elements.

18. According to Passage 2, how are large amounts of X rays associated with black holes?

    (A) Gases being drawn to the black holes emit X rays.

    (B) Black holes attract all types of light except X rays.

    (C) Black holes emit X-ray radiation when they form.

    (D) Black holes absorb all types of light except X rays, which they reflect.

    (E) Scientists send X rays towards potential black holes to detect their presence.

19. According to Passage 2, what is the most likely reason that black holes are called "black" holes?

    (A) They are dark in color.

    (B) They reflect black light.

    (C) Their reflections are very dim, nearly black.

    (D) X rays that signal their presence are similar to black light.

    (E) Their gravity draws in all colors of light, leaving black (absence of light).

20. How does the way scientists use electromagnetic radiation to study objects differ from Passage 1 to Passage 2?

    (A) In Passage 1, the scientist looked at X-ray radiation, while in Passage 2, they looked at visible radiation.

    (B) In Passage 1, the scientist looked at visible radiation, while in Passage 2, they looked at X-ray radiation.

    (C) In Passage 1, the scientist looked at electric radiation, while in Passage 2, they looked at magnetic radiation.

    (D) In Passage 1, the scientist looked at naturally emitted radiation, while in Passage 2, they had to excite the object to see emitted radiation.

    (E) In Passage 1, the scientist had to excite the object to see emitted radiation, while in Passage 2, they looked at naturally emitted radiation.

Holt Physics: Electromagnetic Induction
Improving Sentences

DIRECTIONS: For each question in this section, select the best answer from among the choices given and fill in the corresponding circle on the answer sheet.

Part of each sentence in items 21 and 22 is underlined. Below each sentence are five ways of phrasing the underlined material. Choice A repeats the original phrasing; the other four choices are different. Choose the answer you think produces the most accurate sentence.

21. Electromagnetic waves are transverse waves that travel at the speed of light and are associated with oscillating <u>visual and electric</u> fields.

    (A) visual and electric

    (B) visual and magnetic

    (C) electric and magnetic

    (D) electric and gravitational

    (E) magnetic and gravitational

22. Lenz's law states that the <u>magnetic field of an induced current</u> opposes the change that caused it.

    (A) magnetic field of an induced current

    (B) electric field of an induced current

    (C) electric field of an induced potential

    (D) electric field of an induced resistance

    (E) magnetic field of an induced resistance

Each sentence in items 23 and 24 contains either a single error or no error at all. If the sentence contains an error, choose the one underlined part that must be changed to make the sentence correct. If the sentence is correct, select choice E.

23. The complete electromagnetic spectrum

    ranges from very <u>long-wavelength</u> <u>X rays</u>
    A   B
    to very <u>short-wavelength</u> <u>gamma</u> rays.
    C   D

    <u>No error</u>
    E

24. <u>Generators</u> convert <u>mechanical</u> energy into
    A   B
    <u>electrical</u> energy, while <u>motors</u> convert
    C   D
    electrical energy into mechanical energy.

    <u>No error</u>
    E

Holt Physics: Atomic Physics
Essay

DIRECTIONS: The essay gives you an opportunity to show how effectively you can develop and express ideas. You should, therefore, take care to develop your ideas, present concepts logically and clearly, and use language precisely.

Your essay must be written on your own paper. You may use both sides of a single sheet of notebook paper. You will have enough space if you write on every line, avoid wide margins, and keep your handwriting to a reasonable size. Remember that people who are not familiar with your handwriting will read what you write. Try to write or print so that what you are writing is legible to those readers.

IMPORTANT REMINDERS:
- **A pencil is required for the essay.** An essay written in ink will receive a score of zero.
- **Do not write your essay in your test book.** You will receive credit only for what you write on a single sheet of notebook paper.
- **An off-topic essay will receive a score of zero.**

Think carefully about the concept presented in the following passage and diagram and the assignment below.

The figures below illustrate the photoelectric effect. This observation, first made in the early 20th century, led to a new theory of the nature of light.

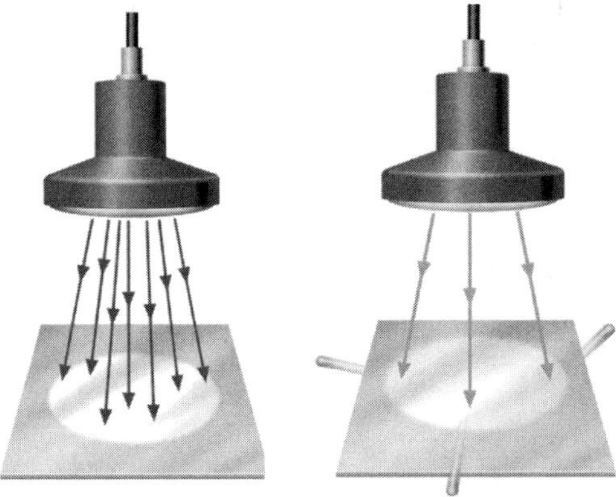

ASSIGNMENT: What is the photoelectric effect? Why does light of only certain frequencies cause electrons to leave the metal plate? Would the effect differ for different metals? Plan and write an essay in which you address these questions. Support your explanation with reasoning and examples taken from your reading, studies, experience, or observations.

Holt Physics: Atomic Physics
Mathematics

DIRECTIONS: In this section, solve each problem using any available space on the page for scratch work. Then decide which of the choices given is best and fill in the corresponding circle on the answer sheet.

NOTES:
1. The use of a calculator is permitted. All numbers used are real numbers.
2. Figures that accompany problems in this test are intended to provide information useful in solving the problems. They are drawn as accurately as possible EXCEPT when it is stated in a specific problem that the figure is not drawn to scale. All figures lie in a plane unless otherwise indicated.

Reference Information

Energy of Light Quantum

$E = hf$

Plank's Constant

$h = 6.63 \times 10^{-34}$ J•s

Maximum Kinetic Energy of a Photoelectron

$KE_{max} = hf - hf_t$

Wavelength of Matter Waves

$\lambda = \dfrac{h}{p} = \dfrac{h}{mv}$

Frequency of Matter Waves

$f = \dfrac{E}{h}$

$1 \text{ eV} = 1.60 \times 10^{-19}$ J

Light Wave Speed Equation

$c = f\lambda$

$c = 3.00 \times 10^{8}$ m/s

1. A photon of UV light has an energy of 3.94 eV. What is the frequency of this photon?

   (A) 2.61×10^{-33} Hz

   (B) 7.61×10^{7} Hz

   (C) 9.51×10^{14} Hz

   (D) 3.83×10^{32} Hz

   (E) 5.94×10^{33} Hz

2. Radiation emitted from hot object reaches its peak at $\lambda = 850$ nm. What is the frequency of this radiation?

   (A) 2.3×10^{-19} Hz

   (B) 1.5×10^{0} Hz

   (C) 3.5×10^{5} Hz

   (D) 5.3×10^{12} Hz

   (E) 3.5×10^{14} Hz

GO ON TO THE NEXT PAGE

Mathematics *continued*

3. How much energy is carried by one quantum of the radiation described in item 2?

   (A) 2.3×10^{-19} eV

   (B) 2.2×10^{-2} eV

   (C) 1.5×10^{0} eV

   (D) 5.3×10^{12} eV

   (E) 3.5×10^{14} eV

4. Photons with energy 7.00 eV strike a metal, producing electrons with a maximum kinetic energy of 4.50 eV. What is the threshold frequency of this metal?

   (A) 4.0×10^{-19} Hz

   (B) 2.5×10^{0} Hz

   (C) 6.03×10^{14} Hz

   (D) 1.09×10^{15} Hz

   (E) 3.77×10^{33} Hz

5. Light of wavelength 214 nm falls on a molybdenum surface, and the photoelectrons are found to have a maximum kinetic energy of 1.2 eV. What is the work function of molybdenum?

   (A) 1.2 eV

   (B) 3.3 eV

   (C) 4.6 eV

   (D) 5.8 eV

   (E) 7.0 eV

6. Given the information in item 5, what is the threshold frequency of molybdenum?

   (A) 2.9×10^{14} Hz

   (B) 8.0×10^{14} Hz

   (C) 1.1×10^{15} Hz

   (D) 1.4×10^{15} Hz

   (E) 1.7×10^{15} Hz

7. With what speed would a 9.0×10^{-14} kg red blood cell have to move if it were to have a wavelength of 2.95×10^{-20} m?

   (A) 0.010 m/s

   (B) 0.25 m/s

   (C) 0.86 m/s

   (D) 1.1 m/s

   (E) 3.0 m/s

8. If the de Broglie wavelength of a hydrogen nucleus ($m = 1.67 \times 10^{-27}$ kg) is equal to 2.24×10^{-15} m, how fast is the hydrogen nucleus moving?

   (A) 1.19×10^{2} m/s

   (B) 2.52×10^{6} m/s

   (C) 1.77×10^{8} m/s

   (D) 1.34×10^{12} m/s

   (E) 1.80×10^{35} m/s

GO ON TO THE NEXT PAGE

Mathematics *continued*

9. What is the de Broglie wavelength of a 425 g soccer ball traveling at 40.0 m/s?

   (A) 3.90×10^{-38} m

   (B) 2.04×10^{-35} m

   (C) 3.90×10^{-35} m

   (D) 6.63×10^{-34} m

   (E) 7.04×10^{-33} m

10. An airplane flying 940 km/h has a de Broglie wavelength of 1.4×10^{-41} m. What is the airplane's mass?

    (A) 1.4×10^{1} kg

    (B) 3.0×10^{4} kg

    (C) 5.0×10^{4} kg

    (D) 1.8×10^{5} kg

    (E) 6.7×10^{6} kg

Questions 11 and 12 are based on the following figure that shows the energy-level diagram for the first five energy levels for mercury vapor. The energy of E_1 is defined as zero. Note: The figure is not to scale.

E_5 ——————————————————— $E = 6.67$ eV
E_4 ——————————————————— $E = 5.43$ eV
E_3 ——————————————————— $E = 4.86$ eV
E_2 ——————————————————— $E = 4.66$ eV

E_1 ——————————————————— $E = 0$ eV

11. What is the frequency of the photon emitted when an electron drops from energy level E_3 to E_1 in a mercury atom?

    (A) 4.83×10^{13} Hz

    (B) 1.12×10^{15} Hz

    (C) 1.17×10^{15} Hz

    (D) 1.31×10^{15} Hz

    (E) 1.61×10^{15} Hz

12. What is the frequency of the photon emitted when an electron drops from energy level E_4 to E_2 in a mercury atom?

    (A) 7.70×10^{-1} Hz

    (B) 1.38×10^{14} Hz

    (C) 1.86×10^{14} Hz

    (D) 1.12×10^{15} Hz

    (E) 1.31×10^{15} Hz

Holt Physics: Atomic Physics
Sentence Completion

DIRECTIONS: For each question in this section, select the best answer from among the choices given and fill in the corresponding circle on the answer sheet.

13. _______ is an increase in the wavelength of the photon scattered by an electron relative to the wavelength of the incident photon.

   (A) Blackbody radiation

   (B) Compton shift

   (C) Photoelectric effect

   (D) Ultraviolet catastrophe

   (E) Uncertainty principle

14. According to the _______, it is impossible to simultaneously determine a particle's position and momentum with infinite accuracy.

   (A) blackbody radiation

   (B) Compton shift

   (C) photoelectric effect

   (D) ultraviolet catastrophe

   (E) uncertainty principle

15. The minimum energy required for an electron to escape from a metal depends on the _______ of the metal.

   (A) absorption spectrum

   (B) blackbody radiation

   (C) Compton shift

   (D) emission spectrum

   (E) threshold frequency

16. An atom's _______ and most of an atom's _______ are contained in its nucleus.

   (A) volume . . mass

   (B) mass . . protons

   (C) neutrons . . protons

   (D) positive charge . . mass

   (E) electrons . . negative charge

Holt Physics: Atomic Physics
Reading Passage

The passage below is followed by questions based on its content. Answer the questions on the basis of what is <u>stated</u> or <u>implied</u> in the passage. For each question in this section, select the best answer from the choices given and fill in the corresponding circle on the answer sheet.

Questions 17–20 are based on the following passage.

Many homes contain a silent danger to children living in them. Paints manufactured 50 years ago contain lead— a toxic metal. If children swallow flakes
Line
5 of this paint, they are at risk of contracting lead poisoning and of developing learning disabilities.

In the past, testing paint flakes for lead required complicated procedures
10 available only at chemical labs or the use of instruments containing radioactive sources.

David Cremers, a scientist at Los Alamos National Laboratory, has plans to
15 change all that with a device called a laser surface analyzer. This device uses a laser to create a tiny spark. The spark is intensely hot, around 5811 K (10 000°F). The spark vaporizes a material to produce
20 atoms that are then excited to emit light.

According to Cremers, "If we take this light from the spark and pass it through a prism to produce a spectrum, we'll see bright emissions in certain
25 colors or regions of the spectrum. Because each element in the periodic table has a unique emission spectrum, by accurately determining the wavelengths of these emissions or the colors of these
30 emissions, we can tell you what elements the material is composed of."

Although the laser surface analyzer was originally created to test walls for toxic paint, it can be used on any surface
35 to test for any elements because each element has a unique emission spectrum. The laser surface analyzer will work on any form of matter: gas, liquid, or solid. The laser pulses are focused by a lens on
40 the sample to form a laser spark. The spark light is collected by a lens and directed to a spectrograph that contains a prism or grating to spectrally disperse the light. The resulting emission spectrum is
45 detected and displayed on the computer screen for analysis.

17. According to the passage, why is it important to completely vaporize the sample as described in lines 16–20?

(A) to create a pure sample of lead

(B) to create a powerful beam of laser light

(C) to thoroughly dry the paint before taking a sample

(D) to remove all of the poisonous substance from the paint

(E) to produce light that shows an identifying emission spectrum

GO ON TO THE NEXT PAGE

Reading Passage *continued*

18. In line 29, the term "colors" refers to

    (A) types of lasers

    (B) pigments in paint

    (C) toxicity of material

    (D) wavelengths of light

    (E) brightness of sparks

19. According to lines 21–31, what can be used to identify an element?

    (A) light reflected off the element

    (B) wavelength of a sample's matter waves

    (C) number of neutrons released by a sample

    (D) emission spectrum from a vaporized sample

    (E) number of photoelectrons released by a sample

20. In this passage, what does the term "spectrograph" in line 42 most likely mean?

    (A) a laser used to vaporize materials

    (B) a paint brush used to apply lead-based paint

    (C) a device that creates an emission spectrum

    (D) a computer used to record measurements

    (E) a printout that shows emission spectrum data

Holt Physics: Atomic Physics
Improving Sentences

DIRECTIONS: For each question in this section, select the best answer from among the choices given and fill in the corresponding circle on the answer sheet.

Part of each sentence in items 21 and 22 is underlined. Below each sentence are five ways of phrasing the underlined material. Choice A repeats the original phrasing; the other four choices are different. Choose the answer you think produces the most accurate sentence.

21. The ultraviolet catastrophe describes <u>an emission spectrum of sunlight</u>.

   (A) an emission spectrum of sunlight

   (B) the type of light emitted by the big bang

   (C) the threshold frequency of most metallic substances

   (D) a theoretical event in which photons move faster than light speed

   (E) a contradiction between classical physics and experimental data

22. In Bohr's model of the atom, electrons radiate energy <u>continuously</u>.

   (A) continuously

   (B) in brief, regular pulses

   (C) from a region known as the electron cloud

   (D) only when they jump from an outer orbit to an inner one

   (E) only when they jump from an inner orbit to an outer one

Each sentence in items 23 and 24 contains either a single error or no error at all. If the sentence contains an error, choose the one underlined part that must be changed to make the sentence correct. If the sentence is correct, select choice E.

23. An <u>absorption spectrum</u> is a diagram or
          A
   graph that indicates the <u>wavelengths</u> of
                              B
   <u>radiant</u> <u>energy</u> that a substance emits.
     C   D
   <u>No error</u>
     E

24. The <u>larger</u> the <u>momentum</u> of an object is,
          A   B
   the <u>smaller</u> its de Broglie <u>wavelength</u>.
          C   D
   <u>No error</u>
     E

Holt Physics: Subatomic Physics
Essay

DIRECTIONS: The essay gives you an opportunity to show how effectively you can develop and express ideas. You should, therefore, take care to develop your ideas, present concepts logically and clearly, and use language precisely.

Your essay must be written on your own paper. You may use both sides of a single sheet of notebook paper. You will have enough space if you write on every line, avoid wide margins, and keep your handwriting to a reasonable size. Remember that people who are not familiar with your handwriting will read what you write. Try to write or print so that what you are writing is legible to those readers.

IMPORTANT REMINDERS:
- **A pencil is required for the essay.** An essay written in ink will receive a score of zero.
- **Do not write your essay in your test book.** You will receive credit only for what you write on a single sheet of notebook paper.
- **An off-topic essay will receive a score of zero.**

Think carefully about the concept presented in the following illustration and the assignment below.

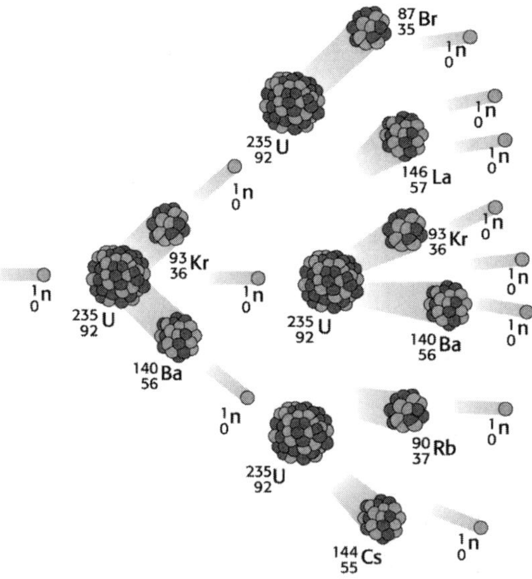

ASSIGNMENT: Describe the nuclear chain reaction illustrated above. What are the starting substances in this process? What substances are produced? What important product allows this reaction to continue exponentially? Plan and write an essay in which you address these questions. Support your explanation with reasoning and examples taken from your reading, studies, experience, or observations.

Holt Physics: Subatomic Physics
Mathematics

DIRECTIONS: In this section, solve each problem using any available space on the page for scratch work. Then decide which of the choices given is best and fill in the corresponding circle on the answer sheet.

NOTES:
1. The use of a calculator is permitted. All numbers used are real numbers.
2. Figures that accompany problems in this test are intended to provide information useful in solving the problems. They are drawn as accurately as possible EXCEPT when it is stated in a specific problem that the figure is not drawn to scale. All figures lie in a plane unless otherwise indicated.

Reference Information

Rest Energy	**Z**	**Isotope**	**Atomic Mass (u)**
$E_R = mc^2$	0	neutron	1.008 665
	1	hydrogen	1.007 825
Binding Energy of a Nucleus	5	boron-10	10.012 936
$E_{bind} = \Delta mc^2$	5	boron-11	11.009 305
	6	carbon-10	10.016 854
Half-life	6	carbon-11	11.011 433
	6	carbon-12	12.000 000
$T_{1/2} = \dfrac{0.693}{\lambda}$	6	carbon-13	13.003 355
	6	carbon-14	14. 003 242
$1 \text{ Ci} = 3.7 \times 10^{10} \text{ s}^{-1}$	15	phosphorus-30	29.978 307
	15	phosphorus-31	30.973 762
	15	phosphorus-32	31.973 907
	88	radium-224	224.020 187
	88	radium-226	226.025 402

1. What is the total binding energy of $^{32}_{15}\text{P}$?

   (A) 31.97 MeV

   (B) 32.26 MeV

   (C) 270.85 MeV

   (D) 282.59 MeV

   (E) 290.77 MeV

2. What is the difference in the binding energies of $^{10}_{5}\text{B}$ and $^{10}_{6}\text{C}$?

   (A) 3.650 MeV

   (B) 4.432 MeV

   (C) 60.320 MeV

   (D) 64.752 MeV

   (E) 125.072 MeV

GO ON TO THE NEXT PAGE

3. What is the binding energy per nucleon of $^{228}_{88}$Ra in MeV?

   (A) 7.16 MeV/nucleon

   (B) 7.64 MeV/nucleon

   (C) 7.94 MeV/nucleon

   (D) 12.45 MeV/nucleon

   (E) 19.80 MeV/nucleon

4. What symbol is missing in the following radioactive-decay formula?

   $^{22}_{11}$Na $\rightarrow$? $+ ^{0}_{1}e + v$

   (A) $^{22}_{12}$Ne

   (B) $^{22}_{9}$Ne

   (C) $^{21}_{10}$Ne

   (D) $^{21}_{11}$Ne

   (E) $^{22}_{10}$Ne

5. What symbol is missing in the following radioactive-decay formula?

   $^{218}_{84}$Po $\rightarrow$? $+ ^{4}_{2}$He

   (A) $^{214}_{82}$Pb

   (B) $^{22}_{82}$Pb

   (C) $^{214}_{86}$Pb

   (D) $^{216}_{82}$Pb

   (E) $^{218}_{84}$Pb

6. Neptunium-239 decays by β^{-} emission to plutonium-239. What is the complete decay formula for this process?

   (A) $^{239}_{93}$Np $\rightarrow ^{235}_{91}$Pu $+ ^{4}_{2}$He

   (B) $^{239}_{93}$Np $\rightarrow ^{238}_{93}$Pu $+ ^{0}_{-1}e + \bar{v}$

   (C) $^{239}_{93}$Np $\rightarrow ^{239}_{94}$Pu $+ ^{0}_{-1}e + \bar{v}$

   (D) $^{239}_{93}$Np $\rightarrow ^{239}_{92}$Pu $+ ^{0}_{1}e + v$

   (E) $^{239}_{93}$Np $\rightarrow ^{240}_{93}$Pu $+ ^{0}_{1}e + v$

7. The half-life of $^{19}_{8}$O is 26.9 s. What is the decay constant for the decay?

   (A) 2.58×10^{-2} s^{-1}

   (B) 3.72×10^{-2} s^{-1}

   (C) 2.69×10^{1} s^{-1}

   (D) 3.88×10^{1} s^{-1}

   (E) 3.88×10^{2} s^{-1}

8. The half-life of $^{234}_{90}$Th is 24.1 d. A thorium-234 sample contains 3.0×10^{8} nuclei. How many thorium nuclei, in curies, will decay per second?

   (A) 2.7×10^{-9} Ci

   (B) 3.3×10^{-7} Ci

   (C) 2.3×10^{-4} Ci

   (D) 2.9×10^{-2} Ci

   (E) 9.9×10^{2} Ci

9. A scientist starts with 1.00×10^{-2} g of a pure radioactive substance and determines 10.0 min later that only 6.25×10^{-4} g of the substance remains. What is the half-life of this substance?

   (A) 0.625 min

   (B) 2.50 min

   (C) 4.00 min

   (D) 6.25 min

   (E) 16.0 min

GO ON TO THE NEXT PAGE

Mathematics *continued*

Questions 10 and 11 are based on the following graph of the decay of a sample of carbon-14.

RADIOACTIVE DECAY

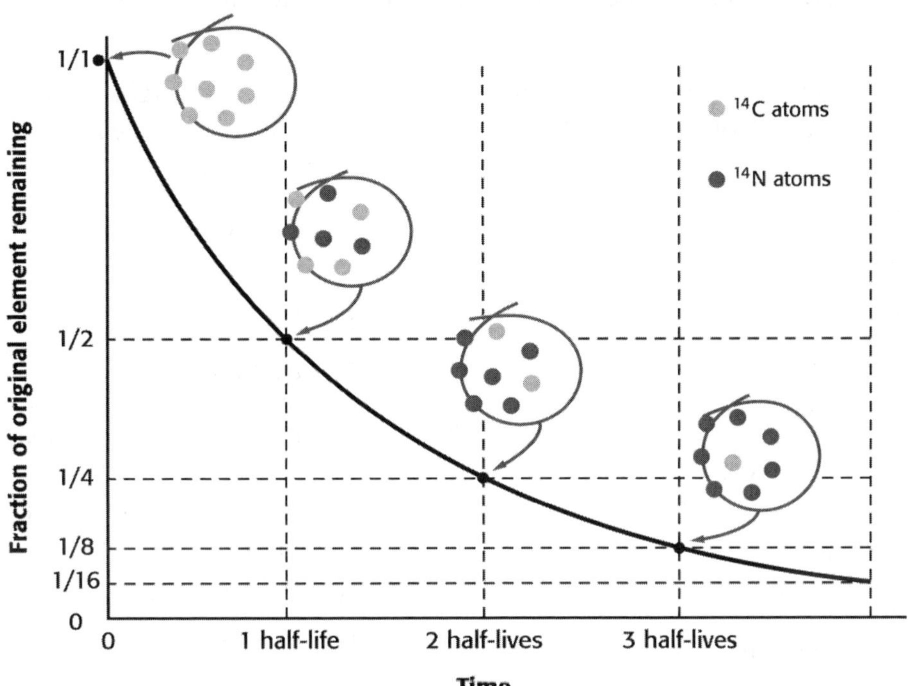

10. What percentage of the sample is carbon-14 after two half-lives?

    (A) 0.25%

    (B) 2%

    (C) 25%

    (D) 50%

    (E) 100%

11. The half-life of carbon-14 is 5715 y. Approximately how old is a sample if only $\frac{1}{8}$ of the original sample is carbon-14?

    (A) approximately 3 y

    (B) approximately 8 y

    (C) approximately 714 y

    (D) approximately 5715 y

    (E) approximately 17 145 y

12. Phosphorus-32 ($^{32}_{15}$P) has a half-life of 14.263 d. A sample contains 1.0×10^{10} phosphorus atoms initially. What is the approximate number of phosphorus atoms that will remain after 71 days?

    (A) about 1.4×10^8 atoms

    (B) about 3.1×10^8 atoms

    (C) about 7.0×10^8 atoms

    (D) about 2.0×10^9 atoms

    (E) about 5.0×10^{10} atoms

Holt Physics: Subatomic Physics
Sentence Completion

DIRECTIONS: For each question in this section, select the best answer from among the choices given and fill in the corresponding circle on the answer sheet.

13. The ______, Z, identifies the element and describes how many protons the nucleus has.

    (A) atomic number

    (B) half-life

    (C) isotope

    (D) mass number

    (E) neutron number

14. Nuclear decay that involves the emission of a helium-4 nucleus is called ______.

    (A) alpha decay

    (B) beta decay

    (C) electron emission

    (D) gamma decay

    (E) positron emission

15. In ______, two light nuclei combine to form a heavier nucleus.

    (A) alpha decay

    (B) beta decay

    (C) fission

    (D) fusion

    (E) gamma decay

16. The fundamental interaction in nature that is responsible for the binding of neutrons and protons into nuclei is called the ______ interaction.

    (A) electromagnetic

    (B) friction

    (C) gravitational

    (D) strong

    (E) weak

Holt Physics: Subatomic Physics
Reading Passages

The passages below are followed by questions based on their content; questions following a pair of related passages may also be based on the relationship between the paired passages. Answer the questions on the basis of what is <u>stated</u> or <u>implied</u> in the passages. For each question in this section, select the best answer from the choices given and fill in the corresponding circle on the answer sheet.

Questions 17 and 18 are based on the following passage, which is part of a letter written in August 1939 by physicist Albert Einstein to President Franklin Roosevelt.

Sir:

    Some recent work by E. Fermi and L. Szilard, which has been communicated to me in manuscript, leads me to expect that the element uranium may be turned into a new and important source of energy in the immediate future. Certain aspects of the situation which have arisen seem to call for watchfulness and if necessary, quick action on the part of the Administration. I believe therefore that it is my duty to bring to your attention the following facts and recommendations.

    In the course of the last four months it has been made probable through the work of Joliot in France—as well as Fermi and Szilard in America—that it may be possible to set up a nuclear chain reaction in a large mass of uranium, by which vast amounts of power and large quantities of new radium-like elements would be generated. Now it appears almost certain that this could be achieved in the immediate future.

17. Given the date of this correspondence, why might Einstein recommend that the American president take "quick action," as indicated in lines 9 and 10?

  (A) In 1939, overuse of nuclear energy in the United States was causing a worrisome shortage of uranium fuel.

  (B) In 1939, the first detonation of a nuclear bomb had caused serious injuries and health risks to Americans.

  (C) In 1939, the world was having an energy crisis that might be solved by the development of nuclear power.

  (D) In 1939, political unrest in Europe gave countries incentive to develop powerful nuclear bombs.

  (E) In 1939, overproduction of nuclear waste was causing dangerous overflow from dump sites.

18. What type of nuclear reaction is Einstein referring to when he uses the term "nuclear chain reaction" in line 18?

  (A) alpha decay

  (B) beta decay

  (C) fission

  (D) fusion

  (E) gamma decay

GO ON TO THE NEXT PAGE

Questions 19 and 20 are based on the following passage and diagram.

"Poets say science takes away from the beauty of the stars—mere globs of gas atoms. Nothing is 'mere.' I too can see
Line the stars on a desert night, and feel them.
5 But do I see less or more?" said American physicist Richard P. Feynman in *The Feynman Lectures on Physics* (1966). Few would doubt that Feynman—a notorious prankster and an amateur artist,
10 musician, and philosopher—understood more than a poet about the stars in the night sky, or at least how the particles that composed them behaved. Feynman jointly won the 1965 Nobel Prize in
15 Physics for his work in the field of quantum electrodynamics, the mathematical study of the interactions between light and electrically charged particles.
20 Throughout his career, Richard Feynman had a reputation as an engaging lecturer, humorous writer, and brilliant physicist. From 1943 to 1945, Feynman worked on the Manhattan Project, Los
25 Alamos National Laboratory's secret research project to build the first atomic bomb. He later developed a way of representing electromagnetic interactions between particles through simple
30 diagrams called Feynman diagrams, such as the one shown at right. His diverse career included participating in a government investigation of the 1986 Challenger space shuttle disaster, in
35 which he famously demonstrated a flaw in one of the shuttle's rubber gaskets.
Born on May 11, 1918 in the suburbs of New York, NY, Feynman was educated at MIT and Princeton and taught

40 at Cornell and Caltech. He married three times and had two children. Feynman died on February 15, 1988, at the age of 69, after years of battling abdominal cancer.

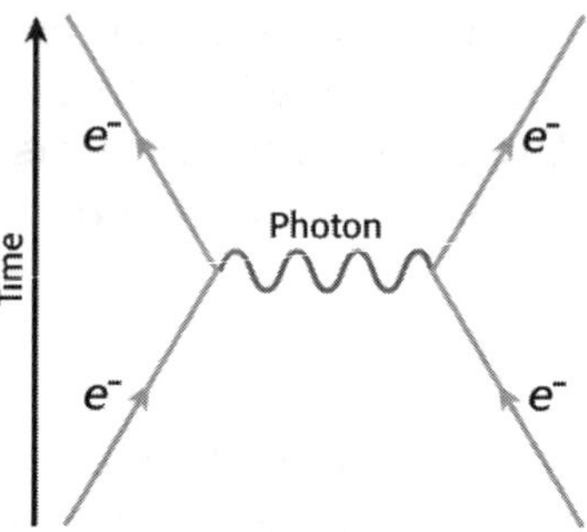

19. According to lines 15–19, quantum electrodynamics can involve interactions
    (A) between stars and planets
    (B) between dark matter and light
    (C) between photons and neutrons
    (D) between photons and electrons
    (E) between neutral particles and light

20. What type of fundamental interaction is illustrated in the Feynman diagram above?
    (A) electromagnetic
    (B) friction
    (C) gravitational
    (D) strong
    (E) weak

Holt Physics: Subatomic Physics
Improving Sentences

DIRECTIONS: For each question in this section, select the best answer from among the choices given and fill in the corresponding circle on the answer sheet.

Part of each sentence in items 21 and 22 is underlined. Below each sentence are five ways of phrasing the underlined material. Choice A repeats the original phrasing; the other four choices are different. Choose the answer you think produces the most accurate sentence.

21. The binding energy of a nucleus is the difference in energy between its <u>number of protons and number of neutrons.</u>

    (A) number of protons and number of neutrons

    (B) number of protons and number of electrons

    (C) number of electrons and number of neutrons

    (D) neutrons when bound and its neutrons when unbound

    (E) nucleons when bound and its nucleons when unbound

22. During nuclear fission, an <u>alpha particle is emitted and a new element is produced.</u>

    (A) an alpha particle is emitted and a new element is produced

    (B) an electron is emitted and a new element is produced

    (C) a positron is emitted and a new element is produced

    (D) a heavy nucleus splits into two lighter nuclei

    (E) two light nuclei combine to form a heavier

Each sentence in items 23 and 24 contains either a single error or no error at all. If the sentence contains an error, choose the one underlined part that must be changed to make the sentence correct. If the sentence is correct, select choice E.

23. <u>Half-life</u> is the time needed for <u>all</u> of the
       A   B
    original <u>nuclei</u> of a sample of a radioactive
           C
    substance to undergo <u>radioactive decay</u>.
                          D

    <u>No error</u>
     E

24. Subatomic particles are either <u>leptons,</u>
                             A
    which include electrons and <u>neutrinos</u>, or
                        B
    <u>hadrons</u>, which are either <u>protons</u> or
      C   D
    baryons. <u>No error</u>
            E

Answer Sheets

Holt Physics
Answer Sheet

CHAPTER 1: The Science of Physics

1	Ⓐ	Ⓑ	Ⓒ	Ⓓ	Ⓔ		**13**	Ⓐ	Ⓑ	Ⓒ	Ⓓ	Ⓔ
2	Ⓐ	Ⓑ	Ⓒ	Ⓓ	Ⓔ		**14**	Ⓐ	Ⓑ	Ⓒ	Ⓓ	Ⓔ
3	Ⓐ	Ⓑ	Ⓒ	Ⓓ	Ⓔ		**15**	Ⓐ	Ⓑ	Ⓒ	Ⓓ	Ⓔ
4	Ⓐ	Ⓑ	Ⓒ	Ⓓ	Ⓔ		**16**	Ⓐ	Ⓑ	Ⓒ	Ⓓ	Ⓔ
5	Ⓐ	Ⓑ	Ⓒ	Ⓓ	Ⓔ		**17**	Ⓐ	Ⓑ	Ⓒ	Ⓓ	Ⓔ
6	Ⓐ	Ⓑ	Ⓒ	Ⓓ	Ⓔ		**18**	Ⓐ	Ⓑ	Ⓒ	Ⓓ	Ⓔ
7	Ⓐ	Ⓑ	Ⓒ	Ⓓ	Ⓔ		**19**	Ⓐ	Ⓑ	Ⓒ	Ⓓ	Ⓔ
8	Ⓐ	Ⓑ	Ⓒ	Ⓓ	Ⓔ		**20**	Ⓐ	Ⓑ	Ⓒ	Ⓓ	Ⓔ
9	Ⓐ	Ⓑ	Ⓒ	Ⓓ	Ⓔ		**21**	Ⓐ	Ⓑ	Ⓒ	Ⓓ	Ⓔ
10	Ⓐ	Ⓑ	Ⓒ	Ⓓ	Ⓔ		**22**	Ⓐ	Ⓑ	Ⓒ	Ⓓ	Ⓔ
11	Ⓐ	Ⓑ	Ⓒ	Ⓓ	Ⓔ		**23**	Ⓐ	Ⓑ	Ⓒ	Ⓓ	Ⓔ
12	Ⓐ	Ⓑ	Ⓒ	Ⓓ	Ⓔ		**24**	Ⓐ	Ⓑ	Ⓒ	Ⓓ	Ⓔ

Holt Physics
Answer Sheet

CHAPTER 2: Motion in One Dimension

1	Ⓐ	Ⓑ	Ⓒ	Ⓓ	Ⓔ	**13**	Ⓐ	Ⓑ	Ⓒ	Ⓓ	Ⓔ
2	Ⓐ	Ⓑ	Ⓒ	Ⓓ	Ⓔ	**14**	Ⓐ	Ⓑ	Ⓒ	Ⓓ	Ⓔ
3	Ⓐ	Ⓑ	Ⓒ	Ⓓ	Ⓔ	**15**	Ⓐ	Ⓑ	Ⓒ	Ⓓ	Ⓔ
4	Ⓐ	Ⓑ	Ⓒ	Ⓓ	Ⓔ	**16**	Ⓐ	Ⓑ	Ⓒ	Ⓓ	Ⓔ
5	Ⓐ	Ⓑ	Ⓒ	Ⓓ	Ⓔ	**17**	Ⓐ	Ⓑ	Ⓒ	Ⓓ	Ⓔ
6	Ⓐ	Ⓑ	Ⓒ	Ⓓ	Ⓔ	**18**	Ⓐ	Ⓑ	Ⓒ	Ⓓ	Ⓔ
7	Ⓐ	Ⓑ	Ⓒ	Ⓓ	Ⓔ	**19**	Ⓐ	Ⓑ	Ⓒ	Ⓓ	Ⓔ
8	Ⓐ	Ⓑ	Ⓒ	Ⓓ	Ⓔ	**20**	Ⓐ	Ⓑ	Ⓒ	Ⓓ	Ⓔ
9	Ⓐ	Ⓑ	Ⓒ	Ⓓ	Ⓔ	**21**	Ⓐ	Ⓑ	Ⓒ	Ⓓ	Ⓔ
10	Ⓐ	Ⓑ	Ⓒ	Ⓓ	Ⓔ	**22**	Ⓐ	Ⓑ	Ⓒ	Ⓓ	Ⓔ
11	Ⓐ	Ⓑ	Ⓒ	Ⓓ	Ⓔ	**23**	Ⓐ	Ⓑ	Ⓒ	Ⓓ	Ⓔ
12	Ⓐ	Ⓑ	Ⓒ	Ⓓ	Ⓔ	**24**	Ⓐ	Ⓑ	Ⓒ	Ⓓ	Ⓔ

Holt Physics
Answer Sheet

CHAPTER 3: Two-Dimensional Motion and Vectors

1	Ⓐ	Ⓑ	Ⓒ	Ⓓ	Ⓔ	**13**	Ⓐ	Ⓑ	Ⓒ	Ⓓ	Ⓔ
2	Ⓐ	Ⓑ	Ⓒ	Ⓓ	Ⓔ	**14**	Ⓐ	Ⓑ	Ⓒ	Ⓓ	Ⓔ
3	Ⓐ	Ⓑ	Ⓒ	Ⓓ	Ⓔ	**15**	Ⓐ	Ⓑ	Ⓒ	Ⓓ	Ⓔ
4	Ⓐ	Ⓑ	Ⓒ	Ⓓ	Ⓔ	**16**	Ⓐ	Ⓑ	Ⓒ	Ⓓ	Ⓔ
5	Ⓐ	Ⓑ	Ⓒ	Ⓓ	Ⓔ	**17**	Ⓐ	Ⓑ	Ⓒ	Ⓓ	Ⓔ
6	Ⓐ	Ⓑ	Ⓒ	Ⓓ	Ⓔ	**18**	Ⓐ	Ⓑ	Ⓒ	Ⓓ	Ⓔ
7	Ⓐ	Ⓑ	Ⓒ	Ⓓ	Ⓔ	**19**	Ⓐ	Ⓑ	Ⓒ	Ⓓ	Ⓔ
8	Ⓐ	Ⓑ	Ⓒ	Ⓓ	Ⓔ	**20**	Ⓐ	Ⓑ	Ⓒ	Ⓓ	Ⓔ
9	Ⓐ	Ⓑ	Ⓒ	Ⓓ	Ⓔ	**21**	Ⓐ	Ⓑ	Ⓒ	Ⓓ	Ⓔ
10	Ⓐ	Ⓑ	Ⓒ	Ⓓ	Ⓔ	**22**	Ⓐ	Ⓑ	Ⓒ	Ⓓ	Ⓔ
11	Ⓐ	Ⓑ	Ⓒ	Ⓓ	Ⓔ	**23**	Ⓐ	Ⓑ	Ⓒ	Ⓓ	Ⓔ
12	Ⓐ	Ⓑ	Ⓒ	Ⓓ	Ⓔ	**24**	Ⓐ	Ⓑ	Ⓒ	Ⓓ	Ⓔ

Holt Physics
Answer Sheet

CHAPTER 4: Forces and the Laws of Motion

1	Ⓐ	Ⓑ	Ⓒ	Ⓓ	Ⓔ	**13**	Ⓐ	Ⓑ	Ⓒ	Ⓓ	Ⓔ
2	Ⓐ	Ⓑ	Ⓒ	Ⓓ	Ⓔ	**14**	Ⓐ	Ⓑ	Ⓒ	Ⓓ	Ⓔ
3	Ⓐ	Ⓑ	Ⓒ	Ⓓ	Ⓔ	**15**	Ⓐ	Ⓑ	Ⓒ	Ⓓ	Ⓔ
4	Ⓐ	Ⓑ	Ⓒ	Ⓓ	Ⓔ	**16**	Ⓐ	Ⓑ	Ⓒ	Ⓓ	Ⓔ
5	Ⓐ	Ⓑ	Ⓒ	Ⓓ	Ⓔ	**17**	Ⓐ	Ⓑ	Ⓒ	Ⓓ	Ⓔ
6	Ⓐ	Ⓑ	Ⓒ	Ⓓ	Ⓔ	**18**	Ⓐ	Ⓑ	Ⓒ	Ⓓ	Ⓔ
7	Ⓐ	Ⓑ	Ⓒ	Ⓓ	Ⓔ	**19**	Ⓐ	Ⓑ	Ⓒ	Ⓓ	Ⓔ
8	Ⓐ	Ⓑ	Ⓒ	Ⓓ	Ⓔ	**20**	Ⓐ	Ⓑ	Ⓒ	Ⓓ	Ⓔ
9	Ⓐ	Ⓑ	Ⓒ	Ⓓ	Ⓔ	**21**	Ⓐ	Ⓑ	Ⓒ	Ⓓ	Ⓔ
10	Ⓐ	Ⓑ	Ⓒ	Ⓓ	Ⓔ	**22**	Ⓐ	Ⓑ	Ⓒ	Ⓓ	Ⓔ
11	Ⓐ	Ⓑ	Ⓒ	Ⓓ	Ⓔ	**23**	Ⓐ	Ⓑ	Ⓒ	Ⓓ	Ⓔ
12	Ⓐ	Ⓑ	Ⓒ	Ⓓ	Ⓔ	**24**	Ⓐ	Ⓑ	Ⓒ	Ⓓ	Ⓔ

Holt Physics
Answer Sheet

CHAPTER 5: Work and Energy

1	Ⓐ	Ⓑ	Ⓒ	Ⓓ	Ⓔ	**13**	Ⓐ	Ⓑ	Ⓒ	Ⓓ	Ⓔ
2	Ⓐ	Ⓑ	Ⓒ	Ⓓ	Ⓔ	**14**	Ⓐ	Ⓑ	Ⓒ	Ⓓ	Ⓔ
3	Ⓐ	Ⓑ	Ⓒ	Ⓓ	Ⓔ	**15**	Ⓐ	Ⓑ	Ⓒ	Ⓓ	Ⓔ
4	Ⓐ	Ⓑ	Ⓒ	Ⓓ	Ⓔ	**16**	Ⓐ	Ⓑ	Ⓒ	Ⓓ	Ⓔ
5	Ⓐ	Ⓑ	Ⓒ	Ⓓ	Ⓔ	**17**	Ⓐ	Ⓑ	Ⓒ	Ⓓ	Ⓔ
6	Ⓐ	Ⓑ	Ⓒ	Ⓓ	Ⓔ	**18**	Ⓐ	Ⓑ	Ⓒ	Ⓓ	Ⓔ
7	Ⓐ	Ⓑ	Ⓒ	Ⓓ	Ⓔ	**19**	Ⓐ	Ⓑ	Ⓒ	Ⓓ	Ⓔ
8	Ⓐ	Ⓑ	Ⓒ	Ⓓ	Ⓔ	**20**	Ⓐ	Ⓑ	Ⓒ	Ⓓ	Ⓔ
9	Ⓐ	Ⓑ	Ⓒ	Ⓓ	Ⓔ	**21**	Ⓐ	Ⓑ	Ⓒ	Ⓓ	Ⓔ
10	Ⓐ	Ⓑ	Ⓒ	Ⓓ	Ⓔ	**22**	Ⓐ	Ⓑ	Ⓒ	Ⓓ	Ⓔ
11	Ⓐ	Ⓑ	Ⓒ	Ⓓ	Ⓔ	**23**	Ⓐ	Ⓑ	Ⓒ	Ⓓ	Ⓔ
12	Ⓐ	Ⓑ	Ⓒ	Ⓓ	Ⓔ	**24**	Ⓐ	Ⓑ	Ⓒ	Ⓓ	Ⓔ

Holt Physics
Answer Sheet

CHAPTER 6: Momentum and Collisions

1	Ⓐ	Ⓑ	Ⓒ	Ⓓ	Ⓔ	**13**	Ⓐ	Ⓑ	Ⓒ	Ⓓ	Ⓔ
2	Ⓐ	Ⓑ	Ⓒ	Ⓓ	Ⓔ	**14**	Ⓐ	Ⓑ	Ⓒ	Ⓓ	Ⓔ
3	Ⓐ	Ⓑ	Ⓒ	Ⓓ	Ⓔ	**15**	Ⓐ	Ⓑ	Ⓒ	Ⓓ	Ⓔ
4	Ⓐ	Ⓑ	Ⓒ	Ⓓ	Ⓔ	**16**	Ⓐ	Ⓑ	Ⓒ	Ⓓ	Ⓔ
5	Ⓐ	Ⓑ	Ⓒ	Ⓓ	Ⓔ	**17**	Ⓐ	Ⓑ	Ⓒ	Ⓓ	Ⓔ
6	Ⓐ	Ⓑ	Ⓒ	Ⓓ	Ⓔ	**18**	Ⓐ	Ⓑ	Ⓒ	Ⓓ	Ⓔ
7	Ⓐ	Ⓑ	Ⓒ	Ⓓ	Ⓔ	**19**	Ⓐ	Ⓑ	Ⓒ	Ⓓ	Ⓔ
8	Ⓐ	Ⓑ	Ⓒ	Ⓓ	Ⓔ	**20**	Ⓐ	Ⓑ	Ⓒ	Ⓓ	Ⓔ
9	Ⓐ	Ⓑ	Ⓒ	Ⓓ	Ⓔ	**21**	Ⓐ	Ⓑ	Ⓒ	Ⓓ	Ⓔ
10	Ⓐ	Ⓑ	Ⓒ	Ⓓ	Ⓔ	**22**	Ⓐ	Ⓑ	Ⓒ	Ⓓ	Ⓔ
11	Ⓐ	Ⓑ	Ⓒ	Ⓓ	Ⓔ	**23**	Ⓐ	Ⓑ	Ⓒ	Ⓓ	Ⓔ
12	Ⓐ	Ⓑ	Ⓒ	Ⓓ	Ⓔ	**24**	Ⓐ	Ⓑ	Ⓒ	Ⓓ	Ⓔ

Holt Physics
Answer Sheet

CHAPTER 7: Circular Motion and Gravitation

1	Ⓐ	Ⓑ	Ⓒ	Ⓓ	Ⓔ	**13**	Ⓐ	Ⓑ	Ⓒ	Ⓓ	Ⓔ
2	Ⓐ	Ⓑ	Ⓒ	Ⓓ	Ⓔ	**14**	Ⓐ	Ⓑ	Ⓒ	Ⓓ	Ⓔ
3	Ⓐ	Ⓑ	Ⓒ	Ⓓ	Ⓔ	**15**	Ⓐ	Ⓑ	Ⓒ	Ⓓ	Ⓔ
4	Ⓐ	Ⓑ	Ⓒ	Ⓓ	Ⓔ	**16**	Ⓐ	Ⓑ	Ⓒ	Ⓓ	Ⓔ
5	Ⓐ	Ⓑ	Ⓒ	Ⓓ	Ⓔ	**17**	Ⓐ	Ⓑ	Ⓒ	Ⓓ	Ⓔ
6	Ⓐ	Ⓑ	Ⓒ	Ⓓ	Ⓔ	**18**	Ⓐ	Ⓑ	Ⓒ	Ⓓ	Ⓔ
7	Ⓐ	Ⓑ	Ⓒ	Ⓓ	Ⓔ	**19**	Ⓐ	Ⓑ	Ⓒ	Ⓓ	Ⓔ
8	Ⓐ	Ⓑ	Ⓒ	Ⓓ	Ⓔ	**20**	Ⓐ	Ⓑ	Ⓒ	Ⓓ	Ⓔ
9	Ⓐ	Ⓑ	Ⓒ	Ⓓ	Ⓔ	**21**	Ⓐ	Ⓑ	Ⓒ	Ⓓ	Ⓔ
10	Ⓐ	Ⓑ	Ⓒ	Ⓓ	Ⓔ	**22**	Ⓐ	Ⓑ	Ⓒ	Ⓓ	Ⓔ
11	Ⓐ	Ⓑ	Ⓒ	Ⓓ	Ⓔ	**23**	Ⓐ	Ⓑ	Ⓒ	Ⓓ	Ⓔ
12	Ⓐ	Ⓑ	Ⓒ	Ⓓ	Ⓔ	**24**	Ⓐ	Ⓑ	Ⓒ	Ⓓ	Ⓔ

Holt Physics
Answer Sheet

CHAPTER 8: Fluid Mechanics

1	Ⓐ Ⓑ Ⓒ Ⓓ Ⓔ	13	Ⓐ Ⓑ Ⓒ Ⓓ Ⓔ
2	Ⓐ Ⓑ Ⓒ Ⓓ Ⓔ	14	Ⓐ Ⓑ Ⓒ Ⓓ Ⓔ
3	Ⓐ Ⓑ Ⓒ Ⓓ Ⓔ	15	Ⓐ Ⓑ Ⓒ Ⓓ Ⓔ
4	Ⓐ Ⓑ Ⓒ Ⓓ Ⓔ	16	Ⓐ Ⓑ Ⓒ Ⓓ Ⓔ
5	Ⓐ Ⓑ Ⓒ Ⓓ Ⓔ	17	Ⓐ Ⓑ Ⓒ Ⓓ Ⓔ
6	Ⓐ Ⓑ Ⓒ Ⓓ Ⓔ	18	Ⓐ Ⓑ Ⓒ Ⓓ Ⓔ
7	Ⓐ Ⓑ Ⓒ Ⓓ Ⓔ	19	Ⓐ Ⓑ Ⓒ Ⓓ Ⓔ
8	Ⓐ Ⓑ Ⓒ Ⓓ Ⓔ	20	Ⓐ Ⓑ Ⓒ Ⓓ Ⓔ
9	Ⓐ Ⓑ Ⓒ Ⓓ Ⓔ	21	Ⓐ Ⓑ Ⓒ Ⓓ Ⓔ
10	Ⓐ Ⓑ Ⓒ Ⓓ Ⓔ	22	Ⓐ Ⓑ Ⓒ Ⓓ Ⓔ
11	Ⓐ Ⓑ Ⓒ Ⓓ Ⓔ	23	Ⓐ Ⓑ Ⓒ Ⓓ Ⓔ
12	Ⓐ Ⓑ Ⓒ Ⓓ Ⓔ	24	Ⓐ Ⓑ Ⓒ Ⓓ Ⓔ

Holt Physics
Answer Sheet

CHAPTER 9: Heat

1	Ⓐ	Ⓑ	Ⓒ	Ⓓ	Ⓔ	**13**	Ⓐ	Ⓑ	Ⓒ	Ⓓ	Ⓔ
2	Ⓐ	Ⓑ	Ⓒ	Ⓓ	Ⓔ	**14**	Ⓐ	Ⓑ	Ⓒ	Ⓓ	Ⓔ
3	Ⓐ	Ⓑ	Ⓒ	Ⓓ	Ⓔ	**15**	Ⓐ	Ⓑ	Ⓒ	Ⓓ	Ⓔ
4	Ⓐ	Ⓑ	Ⓒ	Ⓓ	Ⓔ	**16**	Ⓐ	Ⓑ	Ⓒ	Ⓓ	Ⓔ
5	Ⓐ	Ⓑ	Ⓒ	Ⓓ	Ⓔ	**17**	Ⓐ	Ⓑ	Ⓒ	Ⓓ	Ⓔ
6	Ⓐ	Ⓑ	Ⓒ	Ⓓ	Ⓔ	**18**	Ⓐ	Ⓑ	Ⓒ	Ⓓ	Ⓔ
7	Ⓐ	Ⓑ	Ⓒ	Ⓓ	Ⓔ	**19**	Ⓐ	Ⓑ	Ⓒ	Ⓓ	Ⓔ
8	Ⓐ	Ⓑ	Ⓒ	Ⓓ	Ⓔ	**20**	Ⓐ	Ⓑ	Ⓒ	Ⓓ	Ⓔ
9	Ⓐ	Ⓑ	Ⓒ	Ⓓ	Ⓔ	**21**	Ⓐ	Ⓑ	Ⓒ	Ⓓ	Ⓔ
10	Ⓐ	Ⓑ	Ⓒ	Ⓓ	Ⓔ	**22**	Ⓐ	Ⓑ	Ⓒ	Ⓓ	Ⓔ
11	Ⓐ	Ⓑ	Ⓒ	Ⓓ	Ⓔ	**23**	Ⓐ	Ⓑ	Ⓒ	Ⓓ	Ⓔ
12	Ⓐ	Ⓑ	Ⓒ	Ⓓ	Ⓔ	**24**	Ⓐ	Ⓑ	Ⓒ	Ⓓ	Ⓔ

Holt Physics
Answer Sheet

CHAPTER 10: Thermodynamics

1	Ⓐ Ⓑ Ⓒ Ⓓ Ⓔ	13	Ⓐ Ⓑ Ⓒ Ⓓ Ⓔ
2	Ⓐ Ⓑ Ⓒ Ⓓ Ⓔ	14	Ⓐ Ⓑ Ⓒ Ⓓ Ⓔ
3	Ⓐ Ⓑ Ⓒ Ⓓ Ⓔ	15	Ⓐ Ⓑ Ⓒ Ⓓ Ⓔ
4	Ⓐ Ⓑ Ⓒ Ⓓ Ⓔ	16	Ⓐ Ⓑ Ⓒ Ⓓ Ⓔ
5	Ⓐ Ⓑ Ⓒ Ⓓ Ⓔ	17	Ⓐ Ⓑ Ⓒ Ⓓ Ⓔ
6	Ⓐ Ⓑ Ⓒ Ⓓ Ⓔ	18	Ⓐ Ⓑ Ⓒ Ⓓ Ⓔ
7	Ⓐ Ⓑ Ⓒ Ⓓ Ⓔ	19	Ⓐ Ⓑ Ⓒ Ⓓ Ⓔ
8	Ⓐ Ⓑ Ⓒ Ⓓ Ⓔ	20	Ⓐ Ⓑ Ⓒ Ⓓ Ⓔ
9	Ⓐ Ⓑ Ⓒ Ⓓ Ⓔ	21	Ⓐ Ⓑ Ⓒ Ⓓ Ⓔ
10	Ⓐ Ⓑ Ⓒ Ⓓ Ⓔ	22	Ⓐ Ⓑ Ⓒ Ⓓ Ⓔ
11	Ⓐ Ⓑ Ⓒ Ⓓ Ⓔ	23	Ⓐ Ⓑ Ⓒ Ⓓ Ⓔ
12	Ⓐ Ⓑ Ⓒ Ⓓ Ⓔ	24	Ⓐ Ⓑ Ⓒ Ⓓ Ⓔ

Holt Physics
Answer Sheet

CHAPTER 11: Vibrations and Waves

1	Ⓐ	Ⓑ	Ⓒ	Ⓓ	Ⓔ	**13**	Ⓐ	Ⓑ	Ⓒ	Ⓓ	Ⓔ
2	Ⓐ	Ⓑ	Ⓒ	Ⓓ	Ⓔ	**14**	Ⓐ	Ⓑ	Ⓒ	Ⓓ	Ⓔ
3	Ⓐ	Ⓑ	Ⓒ	Ⓓ	Ⓔ	**15**	Ⓐ	Ⓑ	Ⓒ	Ⓓ	Ⓔ
4	Ⓐ	Ⓑ	Ⓒ	Ⓓ	Ⓔ	**16**	Ⓐ	Ⓑ	Ⓒ	Ⓓ	Ⓔ
5	Ⓐ	Ⓑ	Ⓒ	Ⓓ	Ⓔ	**17**	Ⓐ	Ⓑ	Ⓒ	Ⓓ	Ⓔ
6	Ⓐ	Ⓑ	Ⓒ	Ⓓ	Ⓔ	**18**	Ⓐ	Ⓑ	Ⓒ	Ⓓ	Ⓔ
7	Ⓐ	Ⓑ	Ⓒ	Ⓓ	Ⓔ	**19**	Ⓐ	Ⓑ	Ⓒ	Ⓓ	Ⓔ
8	Ⓐ	Ⓑ	Ⓒ	Ⓓ	Ⓔ	**20**	Ⓐ	Ⓑ	Ⓒ	Ⓓ	Ⓔ
9	Ⓐ	Ⓑ	Ⓒ	Ⓓ	Ⓔ	**21**	Ⓐ	Ⓑ	Ⓒ	Ⓓ	Ⓔ
10	Ⓐ	Ⓑ	Ⓒ	Ⓓ	Ⓔ	**22**	Ⓐ	Ⓑ	Ⓒ	Ⓓ	Ⓔ
11	Ⓐ	Ⓑ	Ⓒ	Ⓓ	Ⓔ	**23**	Ⓐ	Ⓑ	Ⓒ	Ⓓ	Ⓔ
12	Ⓐ	Ⓑ	Ⓒ	Ⓓ	Ⓔ	**24**	Ⓐ	Ⓑ	Ⓒ	Ⓓ	Ⓔ

Holt Physics
Answer Sheet

CHAPTER 12: Sound

1	Ⓐ	Ⓑ	Ⓒ	Ⓓ	Ⓔ		13	Ⓐ	Ⓑ	Ⓒ	Ⓓ	Ⓔ
2	Ⓐ	Ⓑ	Ⓒ	Ⓓ	Ⓔ		14	Ⓐ	Ⓑ	Ⓒ	Ⓓ	Ⓔ
3	Ⓐ	Ⓑ	Ⓒ	Ⓓ	Ⓔ		15	Ⓐ	Ⓑ	Ⓒ	Ⓓ	Ⓔ
4	Ⓐ	Ⓑ	Ⓒ	Ⓓ	Ⓔ		16	Ⓐ	Ⓑ	Ⓒ	Ⓓ	Ⓔ
5	Ⓐ	Ⓑ	Ⓒ	Ⓓ	Ⓔ		17	Ⓐ	Ⓑ	Ⓒ	Ⓓ	Ⓔ
6	Ⓐ	Ⓑ	Ⓒ	Ⓓ	Ⓔ		18	Ⓐ	Ⓑ	Ⓒ	Ⓓ	Ⓔ
7	Ⓐ	Ⓑ	Ⓒ	Ⓓ	Ⓔ		19	Ⓐ	Ⓑ	Ⓒ	Ⓓ	Ⓔ
8	Ⓐ	Ⓑ	Ⓒ	Ⓓ	Ⓔ		20	Ⓐ	Ⓑ	Ⓒ	Ⓓ	Ⓔ
9	Ⓐ	Ⓑ	Ⓒ	Ⓓ	Ⓔ		21	Ⓐ	Ⓑ	Ⓒ	Ⓓ	Ⓔ
10	Ⓐ	Ⓑ	Ⓒ	Ⓓ	Ⓔ		22	Ⓐ	Ⓑ	Ⓒ	Ⓓ	Ⓔ
11	Ⓐ	Ⓑ	Ⓒ	Ⓓ	Ⓔ		23	Ⓐ	Ⓑ	Ⓒ	Ⓓ	Ⓔ
12	Ⓐ	Ⓑ	Ⓒ	Ⓓ	Ⓔ		24	Ⓐ	Ⓑ	Ⓒ	Ⓓ	Ⓔ

Holt Physics
Answer Sheet

CHAPTER 13: Light and Reflection

1	Ⓐ	Ⓑ	Ⓒ	Ⓓ	Ⓔ	**13**	Ⓐ	Ⓑ	Ⓒ	Ⓓ	Ⓔ
2	Ⓐ	Ⓑ	Ⓒ	Ⓓ	Ⓔ	**14**	Ⓐ	Ⓑ	Ⓒ	Ⓓ	Ⓔ
3	Ⓐ	Ⓑ	Ⓒ	Ⓓ	Ⓔ	**15**	Ⓐ	Ⓑ	Ⓒ	Ⓓ	Ⓔ
4	Ⓐ	Ⓑ	Ⓒ	Ⓓ	Ⓔ	**16**	Ⓐ	Ⓑ	Ⓒ	Ⓓ	Ⓔ
5	Ⓐ	Ⓑ	Ⓒ	Ⓓ	Ⓔ	**17**	Ⓐ	Ⓑ	Ⓒ	Ⓓ	Ⓔ
6	Ⓐ	Ⓑ	Ⓒ	Ⓓ	Ⓔ	**18**	Ⓐ	Ⓑ	Ⓒ	Ⓓ	Ⓔ
7	Ⓐ	Ⓑ	Ⓒ	Ⓓ	Ⓔ	**19**	Ⓐ	Ⓑ	Ⓒ	Ⓓ	Ⓔ
8	Ⓐ	Ⓑ	Ⓒ	Ⓓ	Ⓔ	**20**	Ⓐ	Ⓑ	Ⓒ	Ⓓ	Ⓔ
9	Ⓐ	Ⓑ	Ⓒ	Ⓓ	Ⓔ	**21**	Ⓐ	Ⓑ	Ⓒ	Ⓓ	Ⓔ
10	Ⓐ	Ⓑ	Ⓒ	Ⓓ	Ⓔ	**22**	Ⓐ	Ⓑ	Ⓒ	Ⓓ	Ⓔ
11	Ⓐ	Ⓑ	Ⓒ	Ⓓ	Ⓔ	**23**	Ⓐ	Ⓑ	Ⓒ	Ⓓ	Ⓔ
12	Ⓐ	Ⓑ	Ⓒ	Ⓓ	Ⓔ	**24**	Ⓐ	Ⓑ	Ⓒ	Ⓓ	Ⓔ

Holt Physics
Answer Sheet

CHAPTER 14: Refraction

1	Ⓐ	Ⓑ	Ⓒ	Ⓓ	Ⓔ	**13**	Ⓐ	Ⓑ	Ⓒ	Ⓓ	Ⓔ
2	Ⓐ	Ⓑ	Ⓒ	Ⓓ	Ⓔ	**14**	Ⓐ	Ⓑ	Ⓒ	Ⓓ	Ⓔ
3	Ⓐ	Ⓑ	Ⓒ	Ⓓ	Ⓔ	**15**	Ⓐ	Ⓑ	Ⓒ	Ⓓ	Ⓔ
4	Ⓐ	Ⓑ	Ⓒ	Ⓓ	Ⓔ	**16**	Ⓐ	Ⓑ	Ⓒ	Ⓓ	Ⓔ
5	Ⓐ	Ⓑ	Ⓒ	Ⓓ	Ⓔ	**17**	Ⓐ	Ⓑ	Ⓒ	Ⓓ	Ⓔ
6	Ⓐ	Ⓑ	Ⓒ	Ⓓ	Ⓔ	**18**	Ⓐ	Ⓑ	Ⓒ	Ⓓ	Ⓔ
7	Ⓐ	Ⓑ	Ⓒ	Ⓓ	Ⓔ	**19**	Ⓐ	Ⓑ	Ⓒ	Ⓓ	Ⓔ
8	Ⓐ	Ⓑ	Ⓒ	Ⓓ	Ⓔ	**20**	Ⓐ	Ⓑ	Ⓒ	Ⓓ	Ⓔ
9	Ⓐ	Ⓑ	Ⓒ	Ⓓ	Ⓔ	**21**	Ⓐ	Ⓑ	Ⓒ	Ⓓ	Ⓔ
10	Ⓐ	Ⓑ	Ⓒ	Ⓓ	Ⓔ	**22**	Ⓐ	Ⓑ	Ⓒ	Ⓓ	Ⓔ
11	Ⓐ	Ⓑ	Ⓒ	Ⓓ	Ⓔ	**23**	Ⓐ	Ⓑ	Ⓒ	Ⓓ	Ⓔ
12	Ⓐ	Ⓑ	Ⓒ	Ⓓ	Ⓔ	**24**	Ⓐ	Ⓑ	Ⓒ	Ⓓ	Ⓔ

Holt Physics
Answer Sheet

CHAPTER 15: Interference and Diffraction

1	Ⓐ	Ⓑ	Ⓒ	Ⓓ	Ⓔ		**13**	Ⓐ	Ⓑ	Ⓒ	Ⓓ	Ⓔ
2	Ⓐ	Ⓑ	Ⓒ	Ⓓ	Ⓔ		**14**	Ⓐ	Ⓑ	Ⓒ	Ⓓ	Ⓔ
3	Ⓐ	Ⓑ	Ⓒ	Ⓓ	Ⓔ		**15**	Ⓐ	Ⓑ	Ⓒ	Ⓓ	Ⓔ
4	Ⓐ	Ⓑ	Ⓒ	Ⓓ	Ⓔ		**16**	Ⓐ	Ⓑ	Ⓒ	Ⓓ	Ⓔ
5	Ⓐ	Ⓑ	Ⓒ	Ⓓ	Ⓔ		**17**	Ⓐ	Ⓑ	Ⓒ	Ⓓ	Ⓔ
6	Ⓐ	Ⓑ	Ⓒ	Ⓓ	Ⓔ		**18**	Ⓐ	Ⓑ	Ⓒ	Ⓓ	Ⓔ
7	Ⓐ	Ⓑ	Ⓒ	Ⓓ	Ⓔ		**19**	Ⓐ	Ⓑ	Ⓒ	Ⓓ	Ⓔ
8	Ⓐ	Ⓑ	Ⓒ	Ⓓ	Ⓔ		**20**	Ⓐ	Ⓑ	Ⓒ	Ⓓ	Ⓔ
9	Ⓐ	Ⓑ	Ⓒ	Ⓓ	Ⓔ		**21**	Ⓐ	Ⓑ	Ⓒ	Ⓓ	Ⓔ
10	Ⓐ	Ⓑ	Ⓒ	Ⓓ	Ⓔ		**22**	Ⓐ	Ⓑ	Ⓒ	Ⓓ	Ⓔ
11	Ⓐ	Ⓑ	Ⓒ	Ⓓ	Ⓔ		**23**	Ⓐ	Ⓑ	Ⓒ	Ⓓ	Ⓔ
12	Ⓐ	Ⓑ	Ⓒ	Ⓓ	Ⓔ		**24**	Ⓐ	Ⓑ	Ⓒ	Ⓓ	Ⓔ

Holt Physics
Answer Sheet

CHAPTER 16: Electric Forces and Fields

1	Ⓐ	Ⓑ	Ⓒ	Ⓓ	Ⓔ	**13**	Ⓐ	Ⓑ	Ⓒ	Ⓓ	Ⓔ
2	Ⓐ	Ⓑ	Ⓒ	Ⓓ	Ⓔ	**14**	Ⓐ	Ⓑ	Ⓒ	Ⓓ	Ⓔ
3	Ⓐ	Ⓑ	Ⓒ	Ⓓ	Ⓔ	**15**	Ⓐ	Ⓑ	Ⓒ	Ⓓ	Ⓔ
4	Ⓐ	Ⓑ	Ⓒ	Ⓓ	Ⓔ	**16**	Ⓐ	Ⓑ	Ⓒ	Ⓓ	Ⓔ
5	Ⓐ	Ⓑ	Ⓒ	Ⓓ	Ⓔ	**17**	Ⓐ	Ⓑ	Ⓒ	Ⓓ	Ⓔ
6	Ⓐ	Ⓑ	Ⓒ	Ⓓ	Ⓔ	**18**	Ⓐ	Ⓑ	Ⓒ	Ⓓ	Ⓔ
7	Ⓐ	Ⓑ	Ⓒ	Ⓓ	Ⓔ	**19**	Ⓐ	Ⓑ	Ⓒ	Ⓓ	Ⓔ
8	Ⓐ	Ⓑ	Ⓒ	Ⓓ	Ⓔ	**20**	Ⓐ	Ⓑ	Ⓒ	Ⓓ	Ⓔ
9	Ⓐ	Ⓑ	Ⓒ	Ⓓ	Ⓔ	**21**	Ⓐ	Ⓑ	Ⓒ	Ⓓ	Ⓔ
10	Ⓐ	Ⓑ	Ⓒ	Ⓓ	Ⓔ	**22**	Ⓐ	Ⓑ	Ⓒ	Ⓓ	Ⓔ
11	Ⓐ	Ⓑ	Ⓒ	Ⓓ	Ⓔ	**23**	Ⓐ	Ⓑ	Ⓒ	Ⓓ	Ⓔ
12	Ⓐ	Ⓑ	Ⓒ	Ⓓ	Ⓔ	**24**	Ⓐ	Ⓑ	Ⓒ	Ⓓ	Ⓔ

Holt Physics
Answer Sheet

CHAPTER 17: Electrical Energy and Current

1	Ⓐ	Ⓑ	Ⓒ	Ⓓ	Ⓔ	**13**	Ⓐ	Ⓑ	Ⓒ	Ⓓ	Ⓔ
2	Ⓐ	Ⓑ	Ⓒ	Ⓓ	Ⓔ	**14**	Ⓐ	Ⓑ	Ⓒ	Ⓓ	Ⓔ
3	Ⓐ	Ⓑ	Ⓒ	Ⓓ	Ⓔ	**15**	Ⓐ	Ⓑ	Ⓒ	Ⓓ	Ⓔ
4	Ⓐ	Ⓑ	Ⓒ	Ⓓ	Ⓔ	**16**	Ⓐ	Ⓑ	Ⓒ	Ⓓ	Ⓔ
5	Ⓐ	Ⓑ	Ⓒ	Ⓓ	Ⓔ	**17**	Ⓐ	Ⓑ	Ⓒ	Ⓓ	Ⓔ
6	Ⓐ	Ⓑ	Ⓒ	Ⓓ	Ⓔ	**18**	Ⓐ	Ⓑ	Ⓒ	Ⓓ	Ⓔ
7	Ⓐ	Ⓑ	Ⓒ	Ⓓ	Ⓔ	**19**	Ⓐ	Ⓑ	Ⓒ	Ⓓ	Ⓔ
8	Ⓐ	Ⓑ	Ⓒ	Ⓓ	Ⓔ	**20**	Ⓐ	Ⓑ	Ⓒ	Ⓓ	Ⓔ
9	Ⓐ	Ⓑ	Ⓒ	Ⓓ	Ⓔ	**21**	Ⓐ	Ⓑ	Ⓒ	Ⓓ	Ⓔ
10	Ⓐ	Ⓑ	Ⓒ	Ⓓ	Ⓔ	**22**	Ⓐ	Ⓑ	Ⓒ	Ⓓ	Ⓔ
11	Ⓐ	Ⓑ	Ⓒ	Ⓓ	Ⓔ	**23**	Ⓐ	Ⓑ	Ⓒ	Ⓓ	Ⓔ
12	Ⓐ	Ⓑ	Ⓒ	Ⓓ	Ⓔ	**24**	Ⓐ	Ⓑ	Ⓒ	Ⓓ	Ⓔ

Holt Physics
Answer Sheet

CHAPTER 18: Circuits and Circuit Elements

1	Ⓐ	Ⓑ	Ⓒ	Ⓓ	Ⓔ	**13**	Ⓐ	Ⓑ	Ⓒ	Ⓓ	Ⓔ
2	Ⓐ	Ⓑ	Ⓒ	Ⓓ	Ⓔ	**14**	Ⓐ	Ⓑ	Ⓒ	Ⓓ	Ⓔ
3	Ⓐ	Ⓑ	Ⓒ	Ⓓ	Ⓔ	**15**	Ⓐ	Ⓑ	Ⓒ	Ⓓ	Ⓔ
4	Ⓐ	Ⓑ	Ⓒ	Ⓓ	Ⓔ	**16**	Ⓐ	Ⓑ	Ⓒ	Ⓓ	Ⓔ
5	Ⓐ	Ⓑ	Ⓒ	Ⓓ	Ⓔ	**17**	Ⓐ	Ⓑ	Ⓒ	Ⓓ	Ⓔ
6	Ⓐ	Ⓑ	Ⓒ	Ⓓ	Ⓔ	**18**	Ⓐ	Ⓑ	Ⓒ	Ⓓ	Ⓔ
7	Ⓐ	Ⓑ	Ⓒ	Ⓓ	Ⓔ	**19**	Ⓐ	Ⓑ	Ⓒ	Ⓓ	Ⓔ
8	Ⓐ	Ⓑ	Ⓒ	Ⓓ	Ⓔ	**20**	Ⓐ	Ⓑ	Ⓒ	Ⓓ	Ⓔ
9	Ⓐ	Ⓑ	Ⓒ	Ⓓ	Ⓔ	**21**	Ⓐ	Ⓑ	Ⓒ	Ⓓ	Ⓔ
10	Ⓐ	Ⓑ	Ⓒ	Ⓓ	Ⓔ	**22**	Ⓐ	Ⓑ	Ⓒ	Ⓓ	Ⓔ
11	Ⓐ	Ⓑ	Ⓒ	Ⓓ	Ⓔ	**23**	Ⓐ	Ⓑ	Ⓒ	Ⓓ	Ⓔ
12	Ⓐ	Ⓑ	Ⓒ	Ⓓ	Ⓔ	**24**	Ⓐ	Ⓑ	Ⓒ	Ⓓ	Ⓔ

Holt Physics
Answer Sheet

CHAPTER 19: Magnetism

1	Ⓐ	Ⓑ	Ⓒ	Ⓓ	Ⓔ		13	Ⓐ	Ⓑ	Ⓒ	Ⓓ	Ⓔ
2	Ⓐ	Ⓑ	Ⓒ	Ⓓ	Ⓔ		14	Ⓐ	Ⓑ	Ⓒ	Ⓓ	Ⓔ
3	Ⓐ	Ⓑ	Ⓒ	Ⓓ	Ⓔ		15	Ⓐ	Ⓑ	Ⓒ	Ⓓ	Ⓔ
4	Ⓐ	Ⓑ	Ⓒ	Ⓓ	Ⓔ		16	Ⓐ	Ⓑ	Ⓒ	Ⓓ	Ⓔ
5	Ⓐ	Ⓑ	Ⓒ	Ⓓ	Ⓔ		17	Ⓐ	Ⓑ	Ⓒ	Ⓓ	Ⓔ
6	Ⓐ	Ⓑ	Ⓒ	Ⓓ	Ⓔ		18	Ⓐ	Ⓑ	Ⓒ	Ⓓ	Ⓔ
7	Ⓐ	Ⓑ	Ⓒ	Ⓓ	Ⓔ		19	Ⓐ	Ⓑ	Ⓒ	Ⓓ	Ⓔ
8	Ⓐ	Ⓑ	Ⓒ	Ⓓ	Ⓔ		20	Ⓐ	Ⓑ	Ⓒ	Ⓓ	Ⓔ
9	Ⓐ	Ⓑ	Ⓒ	Ⓓ	Ⓔ		21	Ⓐ	Ⓑ	Ⓒ	Ⓓ	Ⓔ
10	Ⓐ	Ⓑ	Ⓒ	Ⓓ	Ⓔ		22	Ⓐ	Ⓑ	Ⓒ	Ⓓ	Ⓔ
11	Ⓐ	Ⓑ	Ⓒ	Ⓓ	Ⓔ		23	Ⓐ	Ⓑ	Ⓒ	Ⓓ	Ⓔ
12	Ⓐ	Ⓑ	Ⓒ	Ⓓ	Ⓔ		24	Ⓐ	Ⓑ	Ⓒ	Ⓓ	Ⓔ

Holt Physics
Answer Sheet

CHAPTER 20: Electromagnetic Induction

1	Ⓐ	Ⓑ	Ⓒ	Ⓓ	Ⓔ	**13**	Ⓐ	Ⓑ	Ⓒ	Ⓓ	Ⓔ
2	Ⓐ	Ⓑ	Ⓒ	Ⓓ	Ⓔ	**14**	Ⓐ	Ⓑ	Ⓒ	Ⓓ	Ⓔ
3	Ⓐ	Ⓑ	Ⓒ	Ⓓ	Ⓔ	**15**	Ⓐ	Ⓑ	Ⓒ	Ⓓ	Ⓔ
4	Ⓐ	Ⓑ	Ⓒ	Ⓓ	Ⓔ	**16**	Ⓐ	Ⓑ	Ⓒ	Ⓓ	Ⓔ
5	Ⓐ	Ⓑ	Ⓒ	Ⓓ	Ⓔ	**17**	Ⓐ	Ⓑ	Ⓒ	Ⓓ	Ⓔ
6	Ⓐ	Ⓑ	Ⓒ	Ⓓ	Ⓔ	**18**	Ⓐ	Ⓑ	Ⓒ	Ⓓ	Ⓔ
7	Ⓐ	Ⓑ	Ⓒ	Ⓓ	Ⓔ	**19**	Ⓐ	Ⓑ	Ⓒ	Ⓓ	Ⓔ
8	Ⓐ	Ⓑ	Ⓒ	Ⓓ	Ⓔ	**20**	Ⓐ	Ⓑ	Ⓒ	Ⓓ	Ⓔ
9	Ⓐ	Ⓑ	Ⓒ	Ⓓ	Ⓔ	**21**	Ⓐ	Ⓑ	Ⓒ	Ⓓ	Ⓔ
10	Ⓐ	Ⓑ	Ⓒ	Ⓓ	Ⓔ	**22**	Ⓐ	Ⓑ	Ⓒ	Ⓓ	Ⓔ
11	Ⓐ	Ⓑ	Ⓒ	Ⓓ	Ⓔ	**23**	Ⓐ	Ⓑ	Ⓒ	Ⓓ	Ⓔ
12	Ⓐ	Ⓑ	Ⓒ	Ⓓ	Ⓔ	**24**	Ⓐ	Ⓑ	Ⓒ	Ⓓ	Ⓔ

Holt Physics
Answer Sheet

CHAPTER 21: Atomic Physics

1	Ⓐ	Ⓑ	Ⓒ	Ⓓ	Ⓔ	**13**	Ⓐ	Ⓑ	Ⓒ	Ⓓ	Ⓔ
2	Ⓐ	Ⓑ	Ⓒ	Ⓓ	Ⓔ	**14**	Ⓐ	Ⓑ	Ⓒ	Ⓓ	Ⓔ
3	Ⓐ	Ⓑ	Ⓒ	Ⓓ	Ⓔ	**15**	Ⓐ	Ⓑ	Ⓒ	Ⓓ	Ⓔ
4	Ⓐ	Ⓑ	Ⓒ	Ⓓ	Ⓔ	**16**	Ⓐ	Ⓑ	Ⓒ	Ⓓ	Ⓔ
5	Ⓐ	Ⓑ	Ⓒ	Ⓓ	Ⓔ	**17**	Ⓐ	Ⓑ	Ⓒ	Ⓓ	Ⓔ
6	Ⓐ	Ⓑ	Ⓒ	Ⓓ	Ⓔ	**18**	Ⓐ	Ⓑ	Ⓒ	Ⓓ	Ⓔ
7	Ⓐ	Ⓑ	Ⓒ	Ⓓ	Ⓔ	**19**	Ⓐ	Ⓑ	Ⓒ	Ⓓ	Ⓔ
8	Ⓐ	Ⓑ	Ⓒ	Ⓓ	Ⓔ	**20**	Ⓐ	Ⓑ	Ⓒ	Ⓓ	Ⓔ
9	Ⓐ	Ⓑ	Ⓒ	Ⓓ	Ⓔ	**21**	Ⓐ	Ⓑ	Ⓒ	Ⓓ	Ⓔ
10	Ⓐ	Ⓑ	Ⓒ	Ⓓ	Ⓔ	**22**	Ⓐ	Ⓑ	Ⓒ	Ⓓ	Ⓔ
11	Ⓐ	Ⓑ	Ⓒ	Ⓓ	Ⓔ	**23**	Ⓐ	Ⓑ	Ⓒ	Ⓓ	Ⓔ
12	Ⓐ	Ⓑ	Ⓒ	Ⓓ	Ⓔ	**24**	Ⓐ	Ⓑ	Ⓒ	Ⓓ	Ⓔ

Holt Physics
Answer Sheet

CHAPTER 22: Subatomic Physics

1	(A)	(B)	(C)	(D)	(E)	**13**	(A)	(B)	(C)	(D)	(E)
2	(A)	(B)	(C)	(D)	(E)	**14**	(A)	(B)	(C)	(D)	(E)
3	(A)	(B)	(C)	(D)	(E)	**15**	(A)	(B)	(C)	(D)	(E)
4	(A)	(B)	(C)	(D)	(E)	**16**	(A)	(B)	(C)	(D)	(E)
5	(A)	(B)	(C)	(D)	(E)	**17**	(A)	(B)	(C)	(D)	(E)
6	(A)	(B)	(C)	(D)	(E)	**18**	(A)	(B)	(C)	(D)	(E)
7	(A)	(B)	(C)	(D)	(E)	**19**	(A)	(B)	(C)	(D)	(E)
8	(A)	(B)	(C)	(D)	(E)	**20**	(A)	(B)	(C)	(D)	(E)
9	(A)	(B)	(C)	(D)	(E)	**21**	(A)	(B)	(C)	(D)	(E)
10	(A)	(B)	(C)	(D)	(E)	**22**	(A)	(B)	(C)	(D)	(E)
11	(A)	(B)	(C)	(D)	(E)	**23**	(A)	(B)	(C)	(D)	(E)
12	(A)	(B)	(C)	(D)	(E)	**24**	(A)	(B)	(C)	(D)	(E)